SHE MAKES POWERFUL *waves*, **BIG, BOLD** *moves*, **AND LISTENS TO THE** *whispers* **OF HER WILD SOUL**

Whisper

From the moment I read the first chapter, I knew I was holding something transformational. Each story had something that I could relate to. I was captivated by the vulnerability, the honesty, and the power behind each woman. When women collectively come together to live out their purpose and their passion, it gives other women the space to take risks, to show up, and to follow their own whisper. Well done, ladies. Thank you for reminding me what courage, passion, and trust look like. The world needs more books like this one.

Shirlee Williams, Spiritual Empowerment Coach /
IG shirleewilliamscoaching / shirleewilliams.com

Every chapter in this book brought me insights and takeaways that are invaluable to my pursuit of growth, and each author's willingness to share a piece of themselves will leave an inspired imprint on your soul. A must-read for women of all ages!

Holly Lo, CEO Oil Babies / IG oil_babies / oilbabies.com

This is truly an inspirational book. *Whisper* supports the reader to stand strong in their power, to trust their inner pull of intuition, and to follow the whispers of that internal guide! I loved curling up on winter evenings to devour these wise women's words and embrace my most authentic, aligned self.

Sarah Norrad, CPC, RYT, MBSR / IG sarah.norrad / sarahnorrad.com

If not now, when?

Something I can 100 percent relate to. *Whisper* hit so close to home and is a beautifully written example of what chasing your dreams can do for you!

Mikaela Woods, CEO - Piper's Closet /
IG piperscloset.ca / piperscloset.ca

Whisper is a must-read book for every woman, at any stage in life. I had goosebumps as I read through the chapters because I saw myself in the journey of every single woman. I've lived through many similar "whispers" and allowed myself to be magnetized to their pull. Every chapter is filled with deep insight and inspiration and will help you build momentum. As a serial entrepreneur and mama of two girls, I felt this exact pull many times before, in life and business, and I will say this: the best thing you can do is leap and trust that the Universe really has your back.

Anna Lozano, Cofounder of Love Powered Co., Coach to female founders /
IG @_annalozano / lovepoweredco.com

Whisper is a refreshing and honest perspective from a group of women who each realize they have to let go of the judgment of friends and family in order to make life choices that have been whispering to them. I saw myself reflected in these pages, and it gave me pause to consider: if they can do it, so can I.

Leith McKay, FindingME podcast host /
IG findingmepodcast / leithmckay.com

So many stories of women sharing their personal experiences. "If Not Now, When?" is a story that resonated with me. We all have dreams, and for many like me, in order to pursue a personal dream, there has to be the right time and there has to be the perfect plan. Having that leap of faith that Agnes and her husband had is inspiring, and it had me revisit the personal dreams I temporarily put aside and am now willing to take.

Sunshine Punzalan / IG shinelily / shinelily.ca

Published in Canada, for Global Distribution

by YGTMedia Co.

www.ygtmedia.co/publishing

To order additional copies of this book:

publishing@ygtmedia.co

Developmental Editing by Tania Jane Moraes-Vaz

Edited by Christine Stock

Book design by Doris Chung

Cover design by Michelle Fairbanks

ePub & Kindle editions by Ellie Silpa

Printed in North America

SHE MAKES POWERFUL *waves*, **BIG, BOLD** *moves*, AND
LISTENS TO THE *whispers* OF HER WILD SOUL

Whisper

SHAYNE HENDERSON | KIRSTI STUBBS

AGNES DALUPANG . ALLISON VILLA . AMY MILNE . JULIE KADEN
KATE WARREN . KELLIE BALES . KYLIE WAECHTER . LAURA FOSTER
MICHELLE RILLI . SABRINA GREER . ASHLEY LOUGHEED
TERI BROWN . KIRTI WHITE . JESSICA JOHNSTONE

Table of Contents

Author Bio

Introduction

Let's first share how *Whisper* came to be. I remember the day Shayne and I reconnected a few months after my move from the city. She was settling into life in Collingwood, Ontario—her renovations had started slowly but then quickly became larger than expected. Just like mine, her to-do list seemed to be growing rather than shrinking. She was supporting her kids' homeschooling and her spouse starting a new business, all while opening her own clinic! I had been thrown headfirst into small-town life in the County mid-winter and was living in the basement living room with my kids while my house was being renovated all around me. I was newly separated and still limping in my Aircast, as I had broken my ankle shortly after the move. Despite all the curveballs Shayne and I were dealing with, our excitement and "rush" of the fresh start were palpable in that conversation. Lots of "YES!!!" from both of us as we recalled our feelings during the transitions. I remember feeling so seen and understood by Shayne. Neither of us had even yet driven back to the city, we were fully immersed in renovations, and we were adjusting to a new lifestyle and new towns. We hadn't looked back! We understood what the other was going through and shared many of the same feelings about moving. We also found comfort in noticing a growing list of women we knew who had already been or were in the process of changing up their lives in major ways. We were in awe of their stories and the leaps they were taking during so much uncertainty. It was so badass and inspiring! Shayne finished our call by saying, "Imagine if there was a collection of stories from these women . . . how wonderful would that be to read?" And just like that, *Whisper* was born.

When I got off the phone with Shayne, I knew she was correct in that these stories needed to be shared. My first collaborative book, *Life, Love, Lemonade,* was set to launch in spring of that year, and as a first-time author, I was nervous and excited. I hadn't considered writing again, nor taking the lead on a new book; however, I couldn't deny that the practice of writing was healing —I wanted to keep going. I reached out to my publisher, Sabrina Greer at YGTMedia Co., and Shayne and I jumped on a call with her to share our idea. Sometimes in the midst of chaos it turns out that adding a creative project to your plate can be exactly what you need to find parts of yourself through the fog, and that is how the seeds of *Whisper* were tended/watered/nourished.

Sabrina was immediately IN for bringing this book to life and got to work on the many pieces behind the scenes that go into birthing books. She, too, had made the leap from city life to small-town living and had even changed her career in the process. She understands what resonates with other women and readers, and before we knew it, we were talking to prospective authors, networking, and doing late-night online searches for women who would hear the call and join us in this coauthored book. That is how the seeds of *Whisper* sprouted.

The women who emerged for this book are truly special. The book evolved as the women came together, and it was beautiful to witness. We are all ages and from all over the world, and we have a diverse set of experiences, skills, and strengths. We didn't all leave big cities for small towns, but each author has made bold moves that have forever changed them. Many of us have experienced loss, change, uncertainty, fear, and crisis. We are resilient. Our stories are unique; however, we share a deep desire to take bold, brave actions to build a life we love. We brought together a beautiful group of women and now *Whisper* is fully rooted and growing.

Our hope for you, our reader, is that your own desires are nourished by our stories and that you can find strength, inspiration, and hope in these pages.

In the beautiful, lush forest, under the surface and in the depths of the tree roots, is a beautiful communication network that makes all this magic possible. The ground of a forest is covered in fungi, moss, and intricate roots from all the low-lying plant life. Working together, they create a vast communication system between the trees we admire. Our hope is that these authors and their vulnerability in sharing their deep inner whispers create a similar connection that speaks to your own intuition and creates a ripple effect of the growth and change that you may be yearning for.

So, as you read this collection of stories, let them wash over you and meet you where you are. Let them nourish what needs to grow inside of you. That is how *Whisper* will create a beautiful forest of brave women standing tall and resilient, each with their own unique stories of growth.

She makes powerful waves, big, bold moves, and listens to the whispers of her wild soul.

SECTION 1

SHAYNE HENDERSON
DR. LAURA FOSTER
TERI BROWN
AGNES DALUPANG
SABRINA GREER

Have you considered how big moments in your life create your before and after?

Each woman has a life or version of themselves that they leave behind as they step into their after. You do not need to have left your career, marriage, or city to feel seen in the pages of *Whisper*. Becoming an adult, ending a relationship, starting a career, changing careers, family life, motherhood, divorce, death, illness, burnout, moving cities, retirement, and so on. Each of us have moments in our life that create a before and after and with them, a loss of self. A loss of a version of ourselves with which we once felt comfortable—a version that is now thrown into newness whether we want it or not. Some moments are complex earthquakes, leaving us shattered and broken open in ways we have never experienced, illuminating parts of us that we are forever changed from seeing. And some are simple, subtle, beautiful shifts, yet still significant to our unique path.

The women in *Whisper* have their own stories of loss and seasons where everything changed. Some made big moves across countries or to small towns, some left communities that they had always known, some wandered away from pain without a clear path, while others intentionally downsized or bought RVs or jumped at new jobs and took off on unexpected adventures. No situation, change, or transformation was the same, and what they experienced was different, yet how they navigated their new experiences was similar. They bravely navigated the dualities so common in our life experiences when we feel different emotions at once—joy and loss, eagerness and fright, being grounded and guarded. They leaned into alignment and took the often challenging road of learning to listen to their intuition. They were bold and resilient, picking themselves up again and again in their search for freedom and peace. They sought out community, learned to ask for help, and allowed themselves to follow their deepest desires by going the way that lights them up. They also embraced the messy parts. They leaned into the idea that whispers don't always make sense and that the timelines we set for ourselves are often nothing like what we expect. They leaned into massive self-trust that they are supported no matter what as long as they listen to their whisper. They embraced the fact that discomfort and growth are part of the process.

They also gave themselves permission, compassion, and grace. Learning to give ourselves permission to let go of something that no longer serves us or grace for where we are—that permission changes everything. Permission for ourselves is equal to having empathy for others—it opens doors to deeper connections, self-love, and liberation.

Before we dig into the beautiful stories in *Whisper*, ask yourself this:

What do you need to give yourself permission to do?

Lean into a change professionally/personally

Let go of a toxic relationship

Stop striving for perfect parent/wife/daughter status

Get more rest

Embrace minimalism

Use your voice

Declutter your entire life

Cancel extracurricular activities

Lean into your heart's desires

Take up that hobby you keep putting off

Write a book

Go for the promotion

Bring in a new boundary

Release your emotions

Burn your shit on the full moon!

Hold space for the thoughts and feelings that are coming up for you. Go slowly. Remember, you are the women of *Whisper*.

Make powerful waves, big, bold moves, and listen to the whispers of your wild soul.

Chapter 1

SLIDING DOORS

SHAYNE HENDERSON

This is your
permission slip
to live a life that
feels true to you,
who you are, your
values, your inner
soul alignment.

@shayne.henderson

Shayne Henderson

Shayne Henderson is a reformed people pleaser (because honestly, who has the time?). She embraces boundaries and loves to solve problems. She is honest to a fault, down-to-earth, fiercely loyal to those she loves . . . and she is an author! She's happiest in the water, she's up for the challenge of homeschooling her inquisitive daughters, and she's married to a triathlete with whom she feels no need to keep up. Shayne is a full-blown body nerd—covering body, mind, and spirit through her bachelor's degree in Kinesiology, her Massage Therapy Certification, and as a Reiki practitioner. She has more than twenty years of experience in women's health, empowering women during pregnancy, birth, and beyond. She is passionate about guiding women to reconnect with themselves physically, emotionally, and mentally, to honor their stories and journey into motherhood, and to embrace their incredible bodies and heal. She holds safe healing spaces for cesarean births (prevention and recovery) and core and pelvic floor issues, and she helps women create more capacity to cope with the emotional labor of motherhood and life. She continues to add layers to her own healing, recognizing that life and health are a continuous journey. You can learn more about what she brings to the world at www.shaynehenderson.com

IG: @SHAYNE.HENDERSON

To Ryan and Rowan,

From the moment you chose me to be your mom,
you have been my inspiration, my greatest teachers,
and the loves of my life. I'm honored to watch you
grow into the incredible women you are meant to
become, and I hope you find inspiration from my
journey. Always embrace your truth and listen to your
inner whispers . . . and get a good night sleep!

All my love,

Mama

Your time is limited, so don't waste it living someone else's life. Don't be trapped by dogma— which is living with the results of other people's thinking. Don't let the noise of others' opinions drown out your own inner voice. And most important, have the courage to follow your heart and intuition.

—Steve Jobs

Everything changes in a moment. One decision. One choice. The only thing you have control over is the direction you take when faced with a fork in the road.

It has been said that on our deathbed we look back and reflect on our lives. *What if we didn't wait? What if we did it while we were still alive? What if we had looked back on the decisions we made and the influences we had and decided to change and follow our heart?*

When I look back on my life, I see many "sliding door" moments— moments when I was presented with a life-altering choice that would forever set me on a different path. Attend university out of province or stay close to home. Travel with a boyfriend or go solo. Stay in the city or move toward the countryside. And there were many more moments I teeter-tottered on the brink of possibilities and expansion. Moments when my heart and intuition wanted me to follow their mesmerizing pull but my brain and logic sobered me up and set me on the safe path. The "right path." But who was it right for? The yearning to discover what was possible never left me. The dreaming never stopped. There never was a moment when I thought "this is everything I have ever wanted."

Life has a way of lulling you into a comfort zone where security and conformity become your foundation despite an inner desire and burning need for more. I've always had a slow flame burning inside, a feeling that I was meant for something different, that I was meant to be somewhere else, living a life that felt challenging yet peaceful and grounded. I allowed my mind to play tricks on me in favor of safety and security and to override my heart- and soul-calling. I grew up with a great sense of responsibility for others: for their expectations and, in a weird way, their happiness. For a long time, it felt like my path was to be the lighthouse in the storm, the dependable one, the constant. I tricked myself into thinking that this is what I wanted . . . perhaps this is where I was meant to be. Over time, I let some of my dreams diminish.

It's a bittersweet pill to swallow. Most of my adult life was shaped and crafted by my logic, something that always tended to outweigh my intuition. And not because my intuition wasn't right. Rather, I wasn't strong enough to trust my intuition at that time. We do the best with what we have and what we know at the time. That was me when I was younger. And when I finally started leaning into my intuition, wading ever so slowly from the shallow to the deep end, knowing that I would always be supported as long as I heard her whispers, I felt freer. This sensation of freedom slowly spilled over, creating greater self-trust, certainty, and the mind-body-soul sovereignty that guides me now.

Do you ever wonder if it's possible to be lost where you are? To that I will say, yes. Very much. I'll be the first to tell you that I used to be judgmental of those who traveled to find themselves. I thought that you should be able to find who you are wherever you are. It turns out I was probably telling myself that to feel better about my own journey. I remember traveling for three months after university and coming back feeling like so much had changed inside of me. I had grown in ways I couldn't describe and had seen things from a completely different perspective. But everything I came back to had seemingly stood still in many ways. The more I felt like I was shouting "I've changed," the more I felt the pressure to fit into the ways of my past self. I think that is when the dreams slowly started slipping away. That is when the fiery inferno started to become a dimly lit flame. Not fully quelled, but not fully there either. The weight of societal expectations—expectations of who everyone else thought I was or what I should do and be—was so overpowering that my visions blurred into theirs. And subconsciously, every time I'd hear that whisper, every time I'd feel that fire rekindling within, I'd douse it with more logic, with other people's plans and paths, with "what I should be doing." I should've followed my heart, but I did the safe thing instead. I started working. I settled down with a friend in an apartment and started growing roots, roots that would, over time, prove to be my biggest challenge.

A continued sense of restlessness showed up in my life. I felt going back to school would give me more options and the travel I craved. I got a sign that I should go to school for massage therapy, one of the key factors being that it would give me a skill that would allow me to work anywhere in the world. I worked as a kinesiologist and personal trainer at the same time, so my clients looked forward to me blending my movement work with hands-on treatment. Logic won out yet again. My intention to travel the world slowly became a forgotten desire as

I settled into establishing my career even more. After all, there was a student loan to pay off and traveling with my new skill seemed frivolous and irresponsible.

And I settled into this life lovingly and willingly with open arms because it was amazing work. Helping people filled my heart on a daily basis, and there were creative challenges in creating wellness plans for people. I had a great and full life with extracurricular activities, lots of friends, and lots of road trips and travel. Interestingly, I was also single at that time, and somehow, despite loving my life, anyone I dated wasn't really local; in fact, several were actually a plane ride away. Like my husband. When I met my husband, he lived in Vancouver, a place I swore I would move to in my twenties. It was a relationship that could rescue me from my own fear of following my heart, that familiar tug that I had known for years. Yet as much as I had dreamed of living out west, my sense and sensibility won out yet again. I was more established in my career, I had a home (he lived on a boat), and I was very embedded in the community. Always up for adventure, he happily moved in with me. Luckily, his adventurous spirit and ideas about moving and starting fresh would help my inner dream blossom. We complemented each other in every way. Every once in a while, he would talk about how fun it would be to move and start fresh, but I saw him gradually shift and immerse himself into *our* cozy life. My cozy life. And mostly because I don't think he ever thought I would move. I was all talk and no action. There were no one-way plane tickets and figuring out where to end up or when to come back. I would talk about it all the time, and on bad days I would look at real estate and dream of what life would be like somewhere else. But then logic, safety, and security would pull me back . . . that is until my whispers were no longer whispers, they were sacred cries and an intense fire I could no longer ignore.

We had planned to explore the idea of moving while on our anniversary trip in Costa Rica in February 2020. We had such an amazing trip. We toyed with the idea of what it would be like to move there and have a rental property, and we even looked into a bodega that was for sale. Of course, sensibility kicked in again: *What would we really do for work? What about school for the girls? Let's just come back and visit again.* So, we came home and, following that whirlwind of an incredible trip, nothing would ever be the same. Within a couple of weeks, I was deemed "nonessential," thanks to the outbreak of COVID-19.

Having my identity tied to and woven so firmly in "what I do" rather than "who I am" meant that for those thirteen weeks of the initial lockdown, I had a lot of things bubbling up. My experience with postpartum depression and anxiety crept back in and my mental health took a dive. Having hard questions and truths to face led me to realize my own wants and needs had become secondary to living the "expected" life—the prescribed life that we all subscribe to: grow up, maybe go to college/university, get a job/career, get married, have kids, settle down. Then work your tail off until "freedom fifty-five" (if you are lucky) or sixty-five, then retire and live your life? Even just writing out this script makes my stomach flip. The idea that this is life for the majority of us, me included! Wholeheartedly too. Yet, how many of us function on autopilot our whole life until we are forced to face an uncomfortable truth? This was my biggest "sliding door" moment.

Looking back, there was nothing that really made me feel like I didn't belong, just little moments of feeling that something was off. Life presented me with a stillness that reconnected me with my intuition. For years, even decades, my life was so full of noise that I silenced my intuition. And how we silence our intuition looks and feels different for each of us. For me, it was the combination of playing it safe, fulfilling expectations of "normal adulting," and being a people pleaser. Yes, on the surface, doing so provided me with a "full" life, but deep within, I felt unfulfilled, like I was playing a role rather than living my life, like I was forever performing instead of simply being.

For years leading up to our decision, I would dream about where we would live and what life would be like. The day finally came when I said it out loud and meant it: "I want to move." We had talked about moving in maybe a year or two. But that day I knew that this, now, was our time. "I don't want to live here anymore" was a quiet but consistent whisper. I wanted to be away from the noise and chaos and listen to my own inner voice for a change. The life that I had built and that we had built together no longer felt like home and that came with a lot. It meant gently letting down those close to me, namely my family. For more than twenty years I had worked with my family in our clinic. It was a safe, secure, and amazing career, one that I was very privileged and grateful to have had. I started at twelve as a receptionist, eventually becoming an in-house kinesiologist after university and then added massage therapy. It was a sacred bond—I treated people who had watched me grow up and knew my whole family. Leaving felt bittersweet, and it wasn't easy to break the news. I really struggled with it, but deep within I knew that I'd struggle even more if I didn't honor this inner wisdom, this intuitive pull to finally do what brings me peace, joy, and fulfillment. I just knew that I needed something new, and different. To be near the water and the forest. Away from all the lights and noise. To have a simpler life in ways I didn't even know I wanted.

My flame was rekindled and then relentless. There was no quelling it. How did this transpire at home, with my relationship and my kids? It was a done deal. I wasn't just browsing listings because of a bad day. No, we were all exploring, dreaming, and openly desiring. We were getting out of this place and moving. Freeing ourselves. Seizing the moment. Listening to all the shivers and goosebumps and experiencing the occasional nausea every time we even thought of moving away from the city. And because we had already been dreaming up places, we knew where that would be. Not the biggest move—just two hours from our old home—but enough of a change to shake up everything and start fresh.

Moving was an adventure filled with a lot of shedding, shedding of what I thought I wanted, what I thought I knew, and recognizing that I had been walking through life detached and disconnected from myself.

From everything I had imagined, it should have been more of a challenge to settle into our new surroundings and to form a community. Yet, it has been the opposite for me. Everything simply flowed with an effortless ease and grace that reaffirmed to me that we made the right move, for us. We were finally living our life. I've been connected with people and relationships that feel like they have been there forever. Maybe you do need the distraction of being displaced to come home to who you truly are—to be your true self and allow yourself to be accepted for that. Reading these words, it might seem like I recreated who I am, but that simply is not true. It often feels like "we have changed" or recreated ourselves because we are no longer wearing the thousand-ton weighted suit of expectations, shoulds, and societal ideals that aren't even true to us to begin with. So no, I didn't recreate myself. Rather, I just shed the weight of every expectation, norm, and ideal that no longer felt aligned, that maybe never felt aligned. Fundamentally, I am the same person, but I am living so much more in my own values.

There's an expression related to pain: "Our body whispers until it screams." I think that's also true of our soul. Anything we don't address, any emotions we suppress or numb out altogether, any desires we don't pay attention to manifest themselves in our bodies. For me, it was anger, anxiety, and adrenal fatigue, things that I am still working on but have improved in the year since we've been living connected back to nature.

Looking back, there have been so many signs that I was meant to do something else and be somewhere other than where I was. But there was also this moral inside of me (which I now know is the rulebook) that *I'm reliable, I do what I say, and I am responsible not just for myself but others too* in ways that weren't mine to bear. Having no real reason to leave isn't enough of a reason to stay. I loved my life in Toronto and leaving came with huge challenges but also huge rewards. There is beauty in leaving the safety of the familiar for the pleasures and possibilities of what calls your heart. Starting two new businesses, homeschooling, creating new connections, and building new friendships have nurtured my soul in ways that haven't happened in a long time. I love our life here in Collingwood. Our work-life balance leans more toward the "life" side. On any day we can explore the trails, hit the beach, go skiing, or embark on new adventures. As much as I love it here, and as much as I am rooted in purpose and alignment here, I now know that when I feel like there's something else out there to explore, I'm not going to ignore the calls. This is your permission slip to leave good for great, to leave ordinary so you can go discover extraordinary, to leave safe and secure for exhilarating and fulfilling. This is your permission slip to live a life that feels true to you, who you are, your values, your inner soul alignment.

Chapter 2

THE SOVEREIGN WOMAN

DR. LAURA FOSTER

We are the
spokeswomen for
a new humanity—
and you are
exactly where you
need to be.

@soulinspiredgurl

Dr. Laura Foster

There is a conversation that exists right below the surface of the conversations we normally have. I've always been the woman most interested in having THAT conversation. I'm Dr. Laura Foster, life and mindset coach to women, retired chiropractor, curator of ROOTS + The Sisterhood, yoga teacher, podcaster, retreat leader, and founder of Soul Inspired Gurl. Simply put, I'm on a mission to lead women back to themselves and transform the way we show up in the world, one bold and courageous step at a time. I am a mom to two amazing boys, united with my partner, Paul, and our blended family of six. You can find us hiking the trails of Kelowna, British Columbia, or hanging on our property along the shores of Kootenay Lake with our dog, Bodhi, and growing community of conscious humans. I spend an inordinate amount of time crafting the perfect cup of coffee and will enthusiastically sing the incorrect words to every song I love. I live for genuine connection, whole-hearted living, and slowing down to savor the sweetness of life.

You can find me dropping my truths daily on the Gram @soulinspiredgurl, weekly on the *Soul Inspired Gurl Podcast*, and forever co-creating the future with the women who are in my signature program ROOTS + The Sisterhood at www.soulinspiredgurl.com

IG: @SOULINSPIREDGURL

I dedicate this chapter to all the women who have been brave enough to offer the world more of who they are. You inspire me. To my greatest teachers and deepest loves, Kyle and Ben.
To Paul—I love our love and the path we walk together.
To my most beloved sister and purveyor of the perfect cup of coffee, Dominica. I love and miss you dearly.

The more you let go, the higher you rise.
—*Yasmin Mogahed*

My career as a chiropractor was a calling—not a job—which was unfortunate, given that I had to walk away from it. For twenty-four years, I lovingly showed up at my clinic, offering healing, knowledge, and support for my community. As my practice and impact grew, it was a gift that continued to grow. I began my chiropractic journey in my early twenties, not knowing that this "career" would help raise me, grant me the latitude to mature, the space to truly express myself, and the freedom to travel, to be sovereign and curious.

I had no way of knowing that the thing I loved the most would be the thing I would need to let burn.

In my early forties, I exited my fifteen-year marriage. When the marriage broke down, I let everything else break down with it. My divorce didn't happen to me, it happened through me, and in that breakdown, I cracked open the very essence of my journey of self-betrayal.

It's confusing when your life is blessed with more privilege than you can ever imagine—and it doesn't feel right or enough. I was filled with deep shame for wanting more than I had been gifted with.

We don't talk about this shame enough.

There is the shame of being blessed with so much and it not being right. The shame of resenting your big, bold life that you spent time, money, and energy creating. The shame of not knowing yourself the way you should . . . and could have, had you been paying attention. The shame of knowing the recovery will come with collateral damage for your kids and important relationships. The shame of being judged and judging yourself.

I sat in the solo, silent fog of shame for a long while. I was curious as to where my twenty-something dreams had come from and exactly when I had abdicated the direction of my life to others' opinions, mainstream ideas, and societal norms.

I thought I had been conscious of my life. I consider myself smart, street savvy, hardworking, and awake to the nuances of humanity, and here I was acknowledging that I had unconsciously created a whole bunch of things, contracts, responsibilities, and identities that weren't really me.

Shouldn't I know better?

I knew I had a lot of unbecoming to do and all of it stemmed from the work I had yet to do within me.

This was the first time in my adult life that I had ever truly taken stock of myself. *Who am I? Why am I here? What do I value? What keeps me up at night? What plants peace in my soul? What do I dream of when no one's watching? Who do I long to meet within myself?*

Who was I if I wasn't the woman I let the world tell me I was?

Success	Grief
Failure	Purpose
Love	Passion
Connection	Fulfillment
Impact	

These topics and questions became the raw and fertile ground for my own awareness and messy awakening.

I felt raw, vulnerable, and deeply inquisitive. I wondered why I had never truly asked myself these questions before. The most intimate questions of my evolution. I had been so busy attaining the societal picture of love, family, success, and happiness that I skipped over the most important relationship in my life.

Me.

The beautiful opportunity that comes from life-altering events like divorce is the chance to rebuild your life in a way that aligns with exactly who you are, and that was my intention. I put everything on the table—my needs, my desires, my values, my relationships, my commitments, my work, my finances, my priorities . . . and the cultivation of my relationship to myself: self-esteem, self-confidence, self-trust, self-advocacy, self-worth, self-discipline, and self-respect. For every yes I spoke, it required a no to something or someone else, and little by little my "new" life started to take shape. I recalibrated it all, one small decision at a time.

It was humbling and oddly freeing.

As I sat on the other side of several years of radical self-awareness and discovery, I started to meet the woman I had hoped was somewhere within me. To others, I still looked like the same confident-ish woman/doc with the career and the two boys she adored who had recently divorced. To me, I was different on every level. Not different like someone else—different like ME. The me that I had never truly met but was within me my entire life.

I felt grounded, peaceful, and proud of the woman I was becoming. I was softer and more powerful in my feminine self. My life felt like a giant exhale in what had been decades of sipping air.

It was time to show up in my newfound potential.

My coming out season was shorter than I would've liked. Seemingly out of nowhere, my body and spirit started a new conversation with me. My energy began dropping and my body became sore. There were many days when I was able to move about my clinic doing patient care with ease, only to sit down at the end of the day and not be able to stand back up. Mornings when I pushed my hands into my thighs to stand tall and let things live on the floor if I dropped them. I knew what to do for back pain, and I doubled down on my already robust self-care regimen.

It helped for a while . . . until it didn't. The Universe, it seemed, had other plans for me.

I reworked my schedule to see fewer patients, and I took twelve weeks of vacation that year . . . and the next, to no avail. No amount of buffering my busy work schedule or stretching my hip flexors addressed what was bubbling up within me. The sad, inconvenient, uncomfortable truth was that it was time for me to leave the work that had been my most influential friend, my muse, my gifted and trusted adviser for my entire adult life. For anyone who has ever felt a deep call to action, it rarely feels like a gift in the moment, and this was no exception.

I resisted.

I pushed back.

I pretended it was unnecessary.

All the while I knew that it was a soul-calling—an up-leveling of my gifts and my path.

The potent truth was that the woman who started this work two decades earlier was no longer here and not because she didn't still love the work or the people. This work was no longer mine to champion.

This transition felt oddly reminiscent of the transformation of my past. Only this time, I felt less certain without the perceived security of my clinic and work.

In a matter of a year, I heeded the call and sold my practice and clinic. I said goodbye to many things and many people, but what I mostly said goodbye to was another layer of old identity and past contracts. I begrudgingly accepted that it was time to move on.

It was February 2020, and I had just finished a month in Spain doing my yoga teacher training. By month end I returned from two sold-out yoga and personal mastery retreats I led in Mexico and Muskoka, Ontario. My coaching practice was taking off, and I was excited for what lay ahead. My plan was to move to British Columbia in September with my partner of five years while our four kids stepped into their lives on their own.

It seemed like a flawless plan.

Before that could happen, roadblocks and redirection began. When the world first came to a grinding halt and the busyness and chaos initially lulled, my intuition pulled the alarm bells. I knew in my soul that my life was about to take an unexpected turn. I began to experience "downloads"—nudges and feelings—that were easy to dismiss and seemingly esoteric, but the journey I had taken in the twelve years prior told me that these were divinely inspired messages. I knew I was being led.

My head told me that I didn't know how to do this.

My heart told me that I have been preparing for this moment my whole life.

> *The quieter you become, the more you are able to hear.*
> *—Rumi*

I stepped back from the buzz around me and got really quiet inside. To keep my sanity and my clarity, I made daily pilgrimages into nature. The further I went, the more I heard. I doubled down on attuning to my inner voice and allowed myself to be extraordinarily curious to what I felt.

As crazy as it sounds, I began to feel the vibration of truth within me and around me. As soon as I acknowledged this, I remembered that as a child I knew what truth felt like, on a visceral and energetic level. I grew up in an environment where sensitivity made me feel safe. It kept me shielded, and when I no longer needed it for that childhood sense of safety, I learned to discount my ability, believing it was a weakness that I needed to overcome.

So, I did.

And now, decades later, it became the very thing that I called back to myself. Like a dial on a dimmer, I turned it up and inward. I allowed my sensitivity to be my wise counsel.

And suddenly I couldn't unhear the truth of my life or that of the world. In one fell swoop, I retired my license, effectively burning the bridge to my old life. I was no longer bound by the regulations and the stipulations of a regulated professional.

I was free to be.

We packed up our family in May 2020 and moved ourselves 2,500 miles across the country. To some, this seemed courageous. To me, it felt necessary. We found a rental house, bought a house soon after, and began to root into our new community. It was time to grow my business into my new life, and I was ready for the familiar feeling of having a daily purpose that felt impactful and fulfilling.

Right away my old self tried to work her way back into my world—goal setting, grinding, productivity, and attainment became familiar feelings. I knew how to create a "successful" business in the way of who I used to be. It was a default setting, and whenever I tried to step back into my former process, I couldn't sustain it. I couldn't hold the masculine energy of who I used to be.

This felt like I was forging a new path without a clear directive.

Sweet soul, that is no longer for you.

Sweet soul, this is meant for you.

Sweet soul, you can choose what feels good.

Sweet soul, what feels like home for your soul?

I needed to go at a slower, more conscious pace, and as I did, my work took form and my business grew. All the while, the world seemed to be getting crazier and crazier. The pandemic wave was in full swing and although I was in it, I wasn't a part of it the way other people seemed to be.

Universal truth and clarity continued to come at me like an unrelenting tidal wave.

The Universe's messages were no longer nuanced and subtle. She was bold, straightforward, and uncompromising. As the information was delivered, I did my best to align with the truth of the world. Along the way I learned to find my feet and stand more solidly in my personal authority in a way that I had never done before.

Who was this woman who was rising up from within me?

When this woman felt called, she spoke. She doesn't second-guess or over think her words. She is more brazen, settled, and sovereign in her voice and her knowing. The less she resisted, the more her message landed with those who were meant to hear it. She accepts that it's not her job to make others okay with her life. Above all, she won't be what you need her to be if it isn't who she is at the core of her being.

This woman is me.

The woman who I have always been but long forgotten.

I know I am not the only woman living in this stream of consciousness. There are many of us awakening to the truth of our lives. There is a deep, meaningful, and lasting purpose to this time, even if our logical brains can't fully grasp the magnitude of it.

I sense that we are done over-celebrating the masculine, power-driven ways of the world. Women are individually and collectively letting go of outdated contracts and limited ways of being and are choosing to communicate and co-create from a place of deep spiritual awareness.

I can no longer speed ahead rather unconsciously in disrespect of my feminine needs and desires.

And something tells me, neither can you.

It's time to fully surrender to the truth of who you are and follow the whispers of your soul. She knows the path of your awakening and will never lead you astray. The power is in the allowing of what needs to fall away, to fall away. You will not be left with nothing. Quite the opposite, sweet soul, you will be standing on the fertile ground of your rise, and Sister, you are not alone.

The world is no longer disposable—nor are we.

We are the spokeswomen for a new humanity—and you are exactly where you need to be.

Chapter 3

STABILITY IN FLOW

TERI BROWN

Whispers from
Source need
quiet and
spaciousness to
be heard.

@heyitsme.terib

Teri Brown

Teri Brown is the proud mom of two grown kids and "Grammi" to one little being and more on the way as *Whisper* is written. She is a certified health and wellness coach, a project manager, and she has obtained a 200-hour RYT (Registered Yoga Teacher) certification. For years she's loved writing about her internal and external journeys, and *Whisper* is her first published work. Her passions are yoga, nature, walks, essential oils, natural health, writing, and adventures big and small with her husband/soul mate. She is always looking forward to the next moments of connection with her kids, grandchild(ren), and mom. Teri believes gratitude changes everything and that meditation and prayer are powerful tools in helping us manifest our reality. She is a lifelong learner, with topics like Ayurveda and naturopathy on her study list.

Currently, Teri is a lead recruiter for Red Seal Recruiting, an established niche business based in Victoria, British Columbia, and she finds this work to be super rewarding. The impact of placing the right person in the right role has a ripple effect into lives, and she's honored to play a part in the process. She's currently learning to lean into her body's wisdom and harness her feminine power, and her plan to write about this journey is in the works. Perhaps a blog? She would absolutely love to support and encourage others in allowing their inner whispers to inspire them to live fully, as this is what will change the world into what it needs to be.

IG: @HEYITSMETERIB

Dedicated to my sweet mom, of course. The one who inspired and stoked my ability to follow my heart and who loves me unconditionally across miles and miles. You are my original road-trip hero and fellow lover of maps. You taught me that I can always uproot and replant and that life is a beautiful adventure if you allow it to be. Xoxo.

The search for security is an illusion . . . and attachment to the known. The known is our past.
Uncertainty, on the other hand, is the fertile ground of pure creativity and freedom. Uncertainty means stepping into the unknown in every moment of our existence. The unknown is the field of all possibilities, ever fresh, ever new, always open to the creation of new manifestations.

–Deepak Chopra, *The Seven Spiritual Laws of Success*

It must have begun shortly after I was born. It feels like it's always been in me—the ability to pick up, pack up, and start over, far, far away. It feels natural.

As a little girl, I always felt like it was just my mom and me. We were a team. As long as we had each other, all was right in the world. She moved us back and forth from California to Ontario, Canada, more than once. A few times, actually. My childhood was a wonderful adventure. Sometimes we were running *from* and other times we were running *toward* something. Cross-continent road trips to new homes and new schools were my normal. Mom sheltered me from the stress, fear, and uncertainty I now know she carried. She held an invisible umbrella that protected me from what must have been storms drenching her, uprooting her, and at times collapsing her with heaviness. I only saw all the colors of the umbrella. I only felt her hand holding mine. I never felt the heaviness she shielded me from.

I think of these early days often, amazed at how my life shifted from *there* to *here*.

Fast-forward to this present moment. . . . Sitting on a rocky point, my pedicure-craving feet earthing into the texture and sacredness of this place. A perfect cup of rich, black coffee from a local roaster has a few sips left. Seagulls soar and squawk, laughing it seems. Two great blue herons glide in sync out of the Arbutus tree to my right.

Since Paul and I arrived here on Vancouver Island, we have toyed with full-time RV living, buying a float home, houseboat, or even a condo or house.

We've been here almost two years now. We've been living in a thirty-six-foot 1997 Dolphin RV the entire time, which was not exactly what I had in mind. More on that a bit later . . .

For the first time in my life, I have no desire to be anywhere other than here. If I didn't have family on the mainland, I would be perfectly happy to never leave this island. Here on the edge of the world, the water lapping shyly, I breathe the sea air deeply, and the birds sing "welcome home" from the ancient trees behind me. Here is where I most feel at peace and one with the elements.

So, how did I get here from way back there?

I can't remember a time when I didn't want to move to a warm climate. I always wanted to experience what it would be like to move somewhere new and start over. Every day would be an adventure. What fun it would be to discover my new favorite grocery store, coffee shop, and walking path! I'd find a new hair stylist by simply asking the stranger

I just met what salon she goes to, complimenting her on her beautiful curly hair. Being new, anywhere, sparks excitement, curiosity, conversation, and connection if you look beyond Google and beyond the screens we hold in the palm of our hand.

My life has always had an aspect of missing someone I love. For most of my childhood, I lived 3,000 miles from my dad and only saw him a few weeks each summer. The tearful goodbyes were a dreaded and regular occurrence. When he and his wife moved from California to Florida, I grew to love it there. It would be my *big move* to the sunshine! I decided that when my kids were self-sufficient, I would make the move from Ontario.

As the potential move approached, I became the lucky winner of the husband lottery! Much like all adventures, we met online (eharmony works!). Our heated romance simmered into a solid, deep friendship, which eventually spurred our romance back on. Hello, intimacy and soul connection. It was a St. Augustine sunrise trip up in a hot air balloon where there was a ring and I said, "Yes!" After seven years of marriage and a whole decade of knowing Paul, I am still floating in the newness and the adventure that is our relationship.

It was June 27, 2015, when we left Ontario for Florida with a U-Haul truck caravan towing one car and the other being driven by one of us. We took turns driving the truck and car combo and the other of our cars. I don't remember what town we stayed in that first night on the road, but I do remember the lightning and thunderstorm. It was one where it felt like it came from the core of the earth and the heavens all at once, with no beginning and no end. All-consuming. Mesmerizing for someone like me who loves watching weather.

My dad died that night. Yes, the very night we crossed the border into the USA en route to be closer to him. To this day, theories of the meaning of him leaving the earth at this precise moment are on replay. His health had been deteriorating for a few months, but we had already made plans to move. The wheels were in motion. It wasn't until a few days before we moved that I realized that he was actually dying. Even then, I don't think I really believed it because of all the times before when he seemed to have cashed in a miracle card.

We settled in Jacksonville, Florida, near my job just north of St. Augustine. As you can imagine, our arrival there was a time of grief, excitement, confusion, and many emotions impossible to define. We had left so many loved ones back in Ontario, and my dad was gone. Everything was new. The loss of my dad brought up lots of inner work for me in a new land without the support systems I was used to. I wasn't my best self, and I was starting a new job. And then there were my kids, in their twenties back in Canada, who had to deal with the loss of their grandpa and their mom moving away all at once. To say mom guilt took a strong hold would be such an understatement.

Paul and I ended up building a great life in Jacksonville, but I often wondered if it was for the long term. I really liked the culture, weather, the cost of living, our beautiful condo, and the sense of freedom of living in America. We lived there for more than four years and for much of that time I missed, with such intensity, having close friendships. I had left some wonderful friends in Ontario, plus my mom, daughter, and son. I used my loneliness as a canvas for building a deeper relationship with myself. I did inner work through writing, meditation, and lots and lots of yoga. I obtained my 200-hour yoga teacher training, then stepped way out of my comfort zone and taught some classes. I became a certified health and wellness coach and also studied project management at the local university and obtained my certification. I love learning and used this space to keep learning and growing.

It was extremely frustrating and saddening that so few came to visit us. *Who wouldn't want to have friends or family in sunny Florida to escape Canadian winters?* As it turns out, almost everyone we knew.

This is when it dawned on me that though I'm energized by newness and adventure, not everyone understands that part of me. The struggle is the relationships. They need to evolve or else they disintegrate. I've realized that though our evolution is inevitable, not everyone welcomes it or embraces it with arms wide open. I don't have control over anything or anyone but myself, and it always comes back to letting go. Inviting others to join us in our move forward, even just to visit, is all we can really do. I'd love nothing more than to stay connected AND honor the whisper that called us forward. Yet that itself can be really hard. It's sad to realize that some relationships lose their depth when they're challenged by miles. It's as if their roots were in the earth rather than in our soul connection. Others flourish quietly in the background, knowing that the connection was never about a place to sit. It was about room to move, to grow. And the thing is, we can't predict which relationships are which, or how they will evolve. We find out as we go.

In 2019 we found out that we had to move back to Canada because of a complication with Paul's US residency. Although we were both saddened, deep down we knew that everything happens for a reason, and this must be for our higher good. Neither of us were thriving, and in looking back now, I know that it was Divine intervention.

We knew the expectation from family and friends was that we would return to Ontario. We contemplated the idea, but we also wondered what it might be like to live in British Columbia. Friends of ours had moved to Vancouver Island in 2016, and we had heard wonderful things about it. We researched, wrestled with both options, and eventually agreed that BC was pulling us. That whisper was far too strong to ignore.

The decision was made, and people were disappointed. There I was again, faced with dodging the guilt darts. Still, I felt that I'd rather live with that than spend the rest of my life wondering *what if. What if we had made the move? What if I had honored my inner wisdom and desire?*

The exciting and unnerving puzzle of moving a three-bedroom home and two cars diagonally across the continent began. What an opportunity to design an epic experience! We wanted to drive, but how would we do it with so many possessions in tow?! We thought about renting an RV and shipping all our stuff. Price checking showed us that buying an older RV and then selling it when we got to BC made more financial sense. And movers are crazy expensive, so U-Haul it was. The two of us, with no experience or knowledge of RVs, began the search. We ended up scoring a 1997 National Dolphin that had never been lived in and had been kept covered in an Italian grandmother's carport in Orlando. Dated is an understatement when it comes to decor, but at least it was clean and had space for us to be reasonably comfortable. Little did we know "Dolphina," as we lovingly named her, would be our home for the next two years. And it's a good thing I didn't know because I would have never agreed to it!

The move was like a game of Tetris. We now had a huge RV, two cars, and a twenty-six-foot U-Haul truck to get more than 2,500 miles across the continent. And we wanted to drive together in Dolphina. The Running Suit Guy came to the rescue! A great friend of ours who runs marathons in a suit as a business (so clearly, he's open to random ideas!) agreed to drive the U-Haul while towing one of our cars to Seattle. We paid his expenses, and he got to visit family on a cross-country road trip. Win-win for all. Paul and I drove Dolphina while towing the other car.

We discovered boondocking and that there is no shame in sleeping in a Walmart parking lot if you're passing through. We had lunch in the Albuquerque diner Walt and Jesse schemed in in *Breaking Bad*. We saw the Grand Canyon and Sedona, and we fell in love with Texas. We spent a night in a lettuce field somewhere near Salinas (yes, really) when our GPS got confused and it was pitch black so we just had to stop. We woke to the sounds of buses bringing in the farm workers, made blueberry French toast, then daylight showed us the way. The memories collected along the way were well worth the move! I don't know that we would have experienced these moments, savored and relished each experience for what it was had we not listened to this whisper. British Columbia was calling our name, but along the way, she helped us grow, heal, evolve even more, and be present and anchored in knowing that we are always supported.

It was the road trip of all road trips! I was in my element as the passenger with my paper maps and colored pens, with our little dog, Tashi Boo Boo the Wonderdog, beside me. We took turns driving the rig, me white-knuckling through the air-suction effect transport trucks created as we passed. I would take a deep breath as I saw them approaching and exhale to the other side. It was a full body and mind experience and oh so exhilarating! That takes courage! I never ever thought I'd be driving an RV cross country! But there we were, available and willing for the entire experience!

The drive through California was special since that's where my roots are. I wanted to show Paul so many special spots that took me back to treasured moments spent with my dad. San Francisco, Carmel-by-the-Sea, the gold country, and that beautiful drive up the coast. Highway signs for familiar streets and towns. Much was so distantly familiar as though from another life or maybe a movie I'd watched. California this time around was not the wild and free, ruggedly beautiful place with the laid-back vibe I remembered. There was a chaotic heaviness and way too much traffic. If I had never been there before, I would have thought this must have been a beautiful place at one time.

Over the border and into BC, we stored our stuff on the mainland and the ferry carried us over to the island. The rugged beauty, clean air, and welcoming people swept us off our feet from day one. We explored rainforests, mountain views, and various RV "resorts." For the last two years, we've lived right by the ocean in our tiny home. Our stuff is now over here on the island, and we visit it from time to time. I discovered a love for simplicity and bold, audacious living. Possessions cannot replace the experience of feeling one with the elements, with nature, with yourself. I've learned to live simply and can't imagine being surrounded by excess. I lack nothing . . . wait, that's not entirely true.

My biggest inner struggle through all of this has been missing my mom and kids. I've always carried this feeling with me. Missing someone intensely is an ache that never goes away. It may be a dull ache, but it's there, often reminding you of its presence, with waves of familiarity, nostalgia, and memories crashing into your being all at once. It's a part of me that has always been. That's all I know. Isn't it interesting how we recreate?

Paul and I traveled back to Ontario for Christmas 2020. We had been thinking of moving back there to be near my mom, daughter, grandson, and soon-to-be son-in-law. For me, it was all about being near them. I wouldn't say it was all guilt, but definitely "The Shoulds" played on repeat in my thought process. I truly missed (and still do) my mom. I love hanging out with her. And I didn't want to be those grandparents who were familiar strangers at every visit. Minute by minute, we convinced ourselves that this was the right thing to do and talked about how wonderful it would be. We told them about our plans at Christmas; though not yet definite, we were working on logistics to see where it led. If all went well, we would be there by June 2021 for Kylie and Steve's wedding. Everyone was so happy. Yet another adventure would await us!

Back here in paradise (yes, really), we had a huge whiteboard to manage all the logistics. There were architectural drawings to build the coach house on our rental property, city approvals, moving and storing our stuff, what to do with Dolphina (we were intent on keeping her in BC, of course, because we knew we would be back), Paul's next career move (I work from home so can be anywhere), and on and on we planned our next move.

And then the sadness set in like a haze. It was as if the artist took a paintbrush and painted over all the bright colors with a fresh coat of gray that was starting to seep into the canvas and dry off. I worked hard to rub off the gray, but of course, that just makes a mess. Here she was again . . . that feeling that I was missing something . . . that I would miss something deeply. Intensely. And I wouldn't be me without it. Except this time it was a place. But it's not just a place. It's where I feel grounded, settled, alive, and like I belong. It's the only place I've ever lived where I didn't have that itch to move somewhere else. I pushed it all down and we pressed forward, intent on doing the "right thing," working profusely to put it all together. But no matter how much we tried, it wasn't coming together, and it would cost thousands of dollars just to get there. We were so stressed. But we felt like we were doing the right thing, so we kept pushing, push, push, push . . . until one day in an outdoor yoga class, my instructor said these words: "Have you ever felt like you keep pushing on the pull door?" *Holy holy, YES, yes, I have! I mean, we've only been trying to do just that with our move to Ontario!* And she went on to talk about allowing, surrendering, and letting go. That was it. Her message settled into my heart with such power and grace. As it turns out, it was a message for Paul too, because it resonated with him just as much. Our plans to move came to a full stop. Our world felt lighter. Except that we dreaded telling our family.

I still remember the conversation when Kylie (also an author in this book) asked how the plans were coming, and I told her that it didn't look like it was going to happen after all. As a parent, it's almost unbearable to disappoint or hurt your child, no matter how old they are. My heart sank as the words spilled out. The gray was starting to take over again. But everything brightened as she explained that they had put their potential move to Calgary on hold because we were coming back to Ontario. *What?!* I didn't know that they were still thinking of it since it had been a while since we'd chatted about it. There are no coincidences, ever, just wild, free whispers that call your name. And this whisper was a bold echo to both my daughter and me that we were meant to always stay connected, closer in proximity, and a move to the west coast was soul-aligned!

Can you imagine that?! Imagine if I paid no attention to my intense feelings and whispers, the pulls that called me to explore, set out and discover where I felt most at peace, at home. Where I felt like I belonged. In that moment I realized that not following my deep inner knowing and listening to "The Shoulds" on repeat was not only blocking me from my best life but also my daughter and her family. And we both almost did just that! Whew, what a relief and release for all of us. When Paul and I settled into the decision that we were staying here because it's right for us, so much fell into place. Everything started coming together almost effortlessly—with ease instead of force. With a divine surrender and allowance for the most aligned opportunities to find us just as much as we desired them too! Paul's career has taken off and he's now in a job that he loves. Kylie and her little family have made the trek to Calgary and are building a wonderful life there.

It was like déjà vu. Back in 2015, when Paul and I left for Florida, there was another trickle-down effect that still gives me chills. My twenty-three-year-old son was not living his best life and had often talked about moving to BC. A few months after we left, Stephen called and told me he had an opportunity to drive to BC with a friend, but he had to leave in a few days. "Should I go?" he asked me. I said to him, "If you don't go, won't you always wonder what would have happened if you did?" I was able to help him to make a life-transforming move that today has "right choice" stamped all over it. *Would he have left if he hadn't seen me do it first? Would he even have reached out to discuss it with me? Maybe, but I like my analysis better!* This moment also taught me and reaffirmed that your relationships are important and your people— whoever they are, wherever they are—should always be rooting for you to thrive, grow, evolve. That they, too, can see the excitement in your whispers, and though they may not always understand why you need to do something, they need to respect it. It doesn't make you selfish, just as it doesn't make them negative. It just ushers you to honor your truth, your bold soul nudges and whispers!

For me, I realized that my whispers come from within me, from yoga teachers, and from trees, water, and birds and songs. They are not selfish because we are all connected. When I accept my own heart's desire without shame and guilt, I allow and encourage others to as well.

I need to make big decisions without any input from others, and I feel empowered to do so. I find it's a much clearer path that way. No well-meaning opinions from the fear filters of those who are often stuck themselves. This often means taking feedback with a grain of salt. Asking yourself whether the person or people delivering their feedback and opinions have a life you desire to emulate or not. I feel like there are some things that are better kept sacred, held within, and guided by our inner whispers. Seek advice and counsel, but do so from those who will expand you, provoke you to explore and grow.

For me, going inward rather than outward creates a clear path forward. Looking outward can paralyze us. Whispers from Source need quiet and spaciousness to be heard. Opinions sprinkled like pebbles from baggage can create doubt in my inner knowing. Protecting our process until our next step is solidly rooted in our hearts and minds keeps it pure and real and guided by divinity within. By the time we share our plan, it's past the point of vulnerability like a bird that's ready to fly. When the news breaks, it is easy to brush away opinions like crumbs off a table.

That inner voice sings clearer and clearer the more we tune in without external noise.

Today we live in a mansion of an RV on the Saanich Peninsula (in Sidney) where I walk through the forest to the ocean daily. Dolphina has been sold to a lovely couple who are thrilled with our colorful upgrades to the decor. Both of my kids, grandson, and son-in-law live in Calgary. It's a short, easy trip.

And then there's my mom. She's still in Ontario, and I pray every day that she will also move west. That's all I can do. I remind myself that it was she who started it all; I mean, she was, after all, the family explorer, seeker, and adventurist, so how could she not? In fact, maybe that's what it has all been about. Maybe she is meant to move west and it couldn't happen unless we were all out here? Prayer hands and crossed fingers.

Out here in BC, there is life everywhere. Everything, and I mean everything, is thriving. There are plants growing out of what look to be dead stumps. Moss, ferns, flowers, and baby trees thrive. Life is tenacious. I wonder if the stump felt abandoned when the tree took the leap? Did the top of the tree that dove into the forest bed as far away as it could reach wonder how it would survive without the stump it had always been supported by? Newness sprouted from the stump and also from the branches that lie as far away as they could dive. Nests of new life created by a moment of separation. Regeneration manifests in moss and ferns. A celebration of creation came from what looked like the death of the tree's connection to the stump. Newness in full color because the tree took the leap. And much like nature's whispers dictate the change in seasons, growth, and life, so do our heart's whispers. It's time to unplug from the chaos and the noise and go within. Listen to her call. . . . Where is she guiding you to? What is she asking of you, from you, for you? Lean in, lean in, lean in.

Chapter 4

IF NOT NOW, WHEN?

AGNES DALUPANG

. . . allow your
logical human
side to lean back
on your soul,
because your
soul's whisper
always has your
back!

@agnes_dal

Agnes Dalupang

Agnes Dalupang is a multi-passionate individual. Former nine-to-five graphic designer turned mom of three household CEO. Wife to a dreamer, living with the motto of "dreams are meant to be lived instead of simply being dreamed about." The words "If not now, when?" pushed Agnes and her husband to leave the city of Toronto to follow their dream and build their own business . . . a modern bed and breakfast in Prince Edward County, Ontario. Her experience in design, her husband's hospitality background, their mutual love for food, traveling, exploring experiences, and the art of entertaining made them truly chase their dream sooner than intended. Although the process is hard, as Agnes is a single mom Monday through Friday because her husband still works in the city and the family only gets to spend time together on the weekend, Agnes is often reminded that as every day passes, they are closer to moving and operating their dream B&B. To keep balanced, Agnes uses her creativity to create decor pieces for the B&B and lots of DIYs, and she spends lots of time cooking and testing future breakfast recipes. She also runs an online Etsy store and sells her one-of-a-kind typography art hoops.

Aside from the everyday work, you can find Agnes hiking the trails with the family, visiting vineyards, dining out and supporting small businesses, and hanging out at the beach until the sun sets.

IG: @AGNES_DAL

For my kids: Mila, Legend, and Atlas. We hope we have
shown you to dream big and do you.

*The very least you can do in your life is to figure
out what you hope for. And the most you can do
is live inside that hope. Not admire it from a
distance but live right in it, under its roof.*
–Barbara Kingsolver, Animal Dreams

Have you ever had similar conversations come up repeatedly, like a
sign that perhaps you should start paying closer attention? I have. For
over ten years, my husband and I would have many roundabout conversations that brought us back to "starting our own business." Selling
everything and living on a deserted island has also been a popular topic.
So popular that while we played the weekly lottery and kept our fingers
crossed, we would dream about the possibilities winning would bring
and what our happy dance would look like. *We would show up for the
last time at work, say "I quit," and dance out the door.* Even if we won
the lottery, "starting our own business" would be on the top of our
list of dreams. One thing we knew for sure was that when it was time
to take that leap and start our own business, it would mean moving
out of the city to somewhere—we just didn't know where yet. Those
early moments when we started to dream together were also when the
Universe began to slowly guide us on our path. Though we hadn't a

single clue about how or when everything would come together, in hindsight, something in me told me to trust the timeline of our life and our desires.

OCTOBER 2019

The conversation slowly started to expand to include potentially partnering up with my husband's parents and buying land together where we could build a small hotel or resort in the Philippines. *Although the thought of living in the tropics excites me, it is so far away from here, the people I know and my family.* At that time, we lived in downtown Toronto in a semidetached home that we planned to renovate and add an addition to one day.

FEBRUARY 2020

I was enjoying maternity leave for the third time. I was also thinking of ways to earn an income working from home, knowing full well that I would not be returning to my graphic design job. I was running an online Etsy store, Harlem's Cottage, selling one-of-a-kind typography art hoops, but it wasn't enough to replace my income before maternity leave. The fear all parents have was very much alive in me those days: *three little children to feed and send to university . . . just how, oh how, will this work? There has to be a way to make this happen, Agnes! I see and hear of so many others doing it, with kids in tow. I just have to get a little creative,* I told myself.

MARCH 2020

The pandemic and lockdown had officially been announced. *I was just about to book a vacation to visit friends in Marrakech, dang it.* My husband, who works in hospitality, had to cancel and postpone upcoming meetings and events at his work. But then things got worse as the media droned on about how things should be back to normal in a few weeks, yet "normal" was nowhere to be found. The weeks turned into months, and by then, my husband, Mauriece, had lost his entire team at work and news about friends and colleagues being laid off or furloughed was the topic du jour. He was left to manage all the work on his own and to work diligently to keep future business on the books when things returned to normal. Every day that passed and as more and more hotels closed down temporarily, we continued to worry. *What if he's next; what are we going to do? How are we going to pay our mortgage and bills?* The familiar whisper chimed in again: *there is another way . . . now is your time.*

OCTOBER 2020

We've got to make a change became a constant thought. We couldn't travel outside of Canada easily so the idea of opening something in the Philippines was no longer feasible. We love the beach so much, though, so being near one was a must. A nonnegotiable. No sooner had I felt this desire to be by water than did Mauriece expand our possibilities with yet another question for me: "How about a 'glamping resort' in Prince Edward County? There aren't enough accommodations in the County. We can find a property with or without a house on it, build domes, and rent them out. We can run the business together and still be close to one of the most beautiful beaches in Ontario!" *That sounds like a great idea!* I had no reservations about being able to do it. It seemed within reach and very possible. We loved the County! We had been visiting for more than twelve years and enjoyed every single trip. The day we had the "lightbulb moment," we started getting really excited about the idea. Right away we started looking at real estate in Prince Edward County. The market was changing quickly and there were not a lot of properties available, but every conversation further propelled us, and things sped up our timeline. Things started becoming real rather quickly. I'm usually one to think things over and not jump into anything too quickly, but this was different; it felt right. My internal voice was loud and positive. *If not now, when? Time has come. We're really doing this!* Things felt very real when we made the phone calls to tell our closest family and friends. Everyone said the same thing: "Love the idea; you guys are gonna do so good with that." The support that came in as more and more people found out was really special. I remember feeling like our news wasn't news to everyone—they heard us following our dream and it just felt right to them as well. It was overwhelming, in the best way, to be so supported by family and friends.

When we broke the news to our kids, they were super excited about being able to have some pets and farm animals. More than anything, they were excited to live close to beautiful beaches. The next step we needed to take was to sell our house, our beloved "Harlem's Cottage," named after our firstborn. As much as we would have loved to keep this city gem, financially it was not possible. The thought of selling our home definitely made my stomach turn in a bittersweet way. So many memories, a life built, a family grown, a life well lived in a home that supported us through every experience of our growth together. We had lived there for six years and brought home two babies; it was filled with so many firsts and so many memories. Our neighborhood was filled with great people, and during COVID, we had become that much closer. We gathered daily at 6:00 p.m. for a sing-along, six feet apart, and we sang, danced, and chatted regardless of weather. These people were a really special part of our lives and community. When we announced our plan to them, they were really sad, but they were happy at the same time. One of them pointed out that everyone who had stayed in this house and moved out went on to become an entrepreneur. *Hmm . . . starting a business has always been a core desire for Mauriece and me and that information is another whisper, yet another sign that we are on an aligned path.*

The sale of our home came quickly; we had a week to declutter and get the house "show ready." It was a lot of late nights. We filled our outdoor shed to the rim and dropped off some bikes and gear with our neighbors. The sign went up. The best decision we made was deciding to move into a hotel for a week. It was way easier than keeping the house clean at all times with three little ones. We tried to keep the kids' routine as normal as we could so that they didn't feel our stress. We were nervous: *What if we don't get any offers?* Even when you are confident in your agent and the market is hot, selling your home is stressful, and we had numbers in our mind we wanted to hit. Yet again, the Universe came through for us: the offers showed up, and just like that we signed the agreement. It felt like we were another step closer to our dream.

NOVEMBER 2020

This time was consumed with looking at property listings. The market was hot in Ontario, and there were many people looking to escape the city with the lockdowns still ongoing. We encountered challenges—some land was protected, and some needed to be rezoned. In our minds, the initial goal was to build our glamping site right by the water, but land by the water was top dollar!

While discouraged by this news, instead of writing off our plans altogether, we did more research and decided a bed and breakfast was the direction we were going to take with one dome structure close to the main house. In those days, picturing myself welcoming guests, making breakfast for them, and seeing people enjoy their stay was very exciting for me. Although the plans were evolving, I could feel the vision in my bones and that feeling helped me know that we were on the right path. This would be the way that anchored us into our new beginnings, a way that would help us earn an income and support our family.

Mauriece and I had a long conversation about how we would run our B&B. We've stayed at B&Bs in the past, and there were things we didn't like. We wanted to attract all age groups and also welcome families (there definitely would be a family suite). We wanted a modern B&B—a place where guests had options about where they dined instead of having a communal space where breakfast, lunch, and dinner is served at a certain time. We wanted to offer experiences and upgrades. We wanted guests to truly have somewhere they could escape without having to leave the province or country given the current events.

Then came the day. We saw a listing for a six-acre property across from a vineyard. There weren't many pictures online, but the listing did state that it was zoned for a bed and breakfast. *Could this be the one?* We decided to drive up to the County to check it out. We drove up the steep driveway, got out of the car, and it felt like we were transported into another time and place. We were in a forest with trees all around, in a beautiful and surreal silence. It was peaceful, and hardly any cars passed by. We explored the land and discovered that it housed a trailer and four bunkies, which were included in the price. We loved it. I pulled a branch from one of the trees and brought it back home with me. It was my way of feeling into the essence of the land and space, my anchor back to this property. There was a lot to think about. We quickly met with our real estate agent and went through further details. The property didn't have water or electricity, so these were some unexpected factors to take into consideration. Mauriece was ready to make an offer right then and there, and I was excited but needed to sleep on it. I knew it was right from the moment I saw it, and I knew we needed to do it. The next day, with butterflies fluttering in our stomachs, we made an offer. The following day, we signed the agreement. I couldn't believe this! It was ours! We were another step closer to our dream. Things were real as ever and moving fast. *What is the next best step?*

DECEMBER 2020

We now owned land, but we had nowhere to live. We needed to find a temporary rental while we built our house. We joked around, saying that if we didn't find anything then we'd live in the trailer. I was really hoping to find something within the same area, so the kids wouldn't have to switch schools twice. Mauriece was going to stay at his job—working from home half the week and the other half from the office in Toronto. A few weeks later, our wonderful real estate agent offered her secondary house to us to rent, and it was in the same school district. We were thrilled and relieved. We now had a home to move to. Everything was falling into place, all in Divine or aligned timing. Now to get things at home sorted and boxed. A few boxes per day made me stay calm and not feel overwhelmed. Christmas was coming and I wanted it to feel special despite the chaos of the upcoming move. I somehow managed to avoid having our home feel like it was packed up. It was a great holiday with our immediate family although we were missing the extended family and many friends.

JANUARY 2021

Our big move. A new year. A fresh start in every way. We were counting down the days and were still busy packing up. Things definitely weren't going as I had imagined—the kids were home doing virtual learning (schools were shut down for the foreseeable future). Mauriece was working from home most days. In between sorting, selling, and donating, I was making the most of my time that was left in the city, as I knew country living would be very different. I needed to prioritize my daily walks to the park to feel my best. I knew I would miss my friends and miss running into people while out and about. I wanted our dreams but moving during the pandemic felt like a bittersweet farewell to a life that had served us up until then. There were a lot of things I'd miss about the big city; however, we were only a two-hour drive away, so we could always slip back into the city for a weekend rendezvous if we wanted.

Just before our move, we decided to visit the County with our contractor to show him the land and discuss the project in detail. We were so excited to get the ball rolling, and there was a lot to do. We learned that we would need an architect to draw up a blueprint for the house. We would also need a water well. Yes, this dream of ours would need a lot of things, yet something told me that we would always be supported, just as we had been so far.

Moving day arrived. I couldn't believe that it was time to say goodbye to the city that held us as we grew together as individuals, then as a couple, and then as a growing family. It was time to say goodbye to this part of our lives, knowing that home is a place that is found within ourselves and our loved ones instead of in a brick-and-mortar house. Dreams are meant to be lived instead of simply being dreamed about. Whispers are meant to be followed, especially if they are something you cannot stop thinking about.

FALL 2021

Hello, Prince Edward County, we are so happy to find a home on this beautiful land. We cannot wait to raise our kids here and slow down a bit. We cannot wait to experience all that you have to offer and to spend more time together as a family. The transition is not all rainbows and unicorns; it's hard.

In July 2021, Mauriece went back to working from the city office full time. I was now momming solo Monday to Friday, and we only got to spend time together as a family on the weekend. We'd never been apart like this, but it's a sacrifice we needed to get through. We reminded ourselves often that with each passing day, we were getting closer to moving into our dream home and operating our B&B and dream business. We were very intentional with our time together, making memories, enjoying our new community, and visiting the beaches all year round.

We named our B&B InnAtLast: a humbling experience that allows you to feel at home away from home, where you can unplug and unwind from your every day, and where you can immerse yourself in the sensation and feeling that you're here and you've finally made it . . . at last. InnAtLast Bed and Breakfast will open in 2022. We are so excited to have you stay with us.

If you are ever wondering which way to go when faced with a crossroad in life, go the way that lights you up most. Your dreams will find a way for you if you are willing to believe in them and never give up. Your whispers will continue to lead you and support you as long as you, too, know that you are always supported, that there is no way you can "mess" anything up. It's okay to feel fear and worry. You are human, after all. But once in a while, allow your logical human side to lean back on your soul, because your soul's whisper always has your back! She had ours.

Chapter 5

CHOOSE YOUR OWN ADVENTURE

SABRINA GREER

Trust the direction;
even if there's
an undercurrent
or a patch of
stagnancy, your
river will always
lead you home.

@sabrina.greer.2.0

Sabrina Greer

Sabrina Greer is lovingly known as "The Book Doula" in her circles for her work "birthing brain babies," also known as books. She is a serial entrepreneur, an 8x best-selling author, international publisher, mentor to authors, and the founder of YGTMedia Company, a boutique blended publishing house supporting purpose-driven humans. She has turned hundreds of aspiring writers into best-selling authors through a collaborative and educational approach. A born leader, Sabrina, even from a young age, knew she would teach and mentor on some level when she grew up.

Sabrina holds a bachelor's degree in developmental psychology and early childhood education and is a certified life coach and NLP practitioner, all of which strongly support her mission to empower and inspire others. When she's not in "the books," you will likely find her off exploring in nature, tending to her seventy-acre farmstead in the woods, being a mom to her three sons, four fur babies and dozens of feather babies, and consistently choosing her own adventures!

IG: @SABRINAGREER2.0

To all the beautiful humans out there feeling like they have no choice, know that you always do, no matter what. To my person, the one who supports my crazy ideas and only quietly judges, thank you for your unwavering trust in me. To my boys, Oliver, Sterling, and Walker, may you always follow your souls' nudges and listen to the whispers of your heart.

*As you imagine and visualize and verbalize
your new story, in time you will believe the new
story, and when that happens, the evidence will
flow swiftly into your experience.*

–Abraham Hicks

Do you believe in fate? You know, that power beyond our control that is believed to determine what happens? What do you believe? Are our paths predetermined? Is the fate of our lives already written in universal scripture somewhere? Or is it our "job" as humans to tap into the "signs" and follow our destiny accordingly? Are we supposed to make our own fate? Or can we simply sit back with our feet up and watch the life we are meant for unfold as it's supposed to?

Ever since I can remember, I've been fascinated by the idea that we can control our fate and that life is really a series of **choices**. As a child, I was obsessed with those *Choose Your Own Adventure* novels. The notion that our choices could drastically impact the outcome really excited me. That by leaning into our intuition, what we choose to do becomes our destiny. I've always found it challenging to articulate my thoughts and beliefs around "destiny" or "fate" or even "God" for that matter. I imagine this is because of the internal tug-of-war between my A-type, logical-brained personality and my eternal optimist, empath heart. I believe society conditions us from a young age to believe that *the harder we work for things, the more we can achieve, and the more success we will accrue.* I was no exception.

I grew up in a middle-class family, an only child to a blue-collar working father and a traditional housewife mother, until my parents decided to foster. I was four years old when I became a big sister to dozens of children in a short time. I loved being a big sis, but it kept my parents extremely busy. My dad worked the graveyard shift at General Motors and hated every minute of it. When he was home he was usually sleeping, and my mom was always running around like a chicken with her head cut off, having between three to six mouths to feed at any given time. I'm not entirely sure where or when I acquired my motivation and desire for a bigger life, as not one moment in time stands out more than another. I just knew I never wanted to settle or live life like it didn't matter. *Did it mean more money? Not necessarily. A bigger house? My parents' house was huge, so no. A fancy car? Cars aren't really my thing.* I didn't yet know. My childhood home was always full of love, and we never went without our basic needs met. Still, I had an indescribable flame that burned deep within my soul, yearning for more than the mundane and "supposed to's."

There is a fine balance between greed and desire, isn't there? How much do we yearn for something because we deeply desire it and how much is programming of what we think we "should" have due to image? The narrative goes something like this: Do well in school so you can go to university. Go to university so you can get that corporate job. Get that corporate job and climb that corporate ladder so you can have that fancy house and provide for your family. Work that corporate job for forty-plus years and put in lots of overtime so you can afford the mortgage on said fancy house, but you'll likely have to sacrifice spending time with that family. *Sound familiar?*

Hustle culture is real and toxic, and it's a plague on our generation, if you ask me. This attachment we have to a never-ending grind is exhausting and so deeply woven into our self-worth. We are conditioned to think we need to swim upstream, like the salmon, and we are encouraged to continually behave this way until we can retire some forty-plus years later.

Confession: I used to be part of the **Hustle Club**. I worked a corporate nine-to-five, which was actually an eight-to-ten on good days. The beverage alcohol industry came with its ups and downs. I worked around the clock, weekends, late nights, and early mornings. When I wasn't *physically* at work, my mind was still *at work*—always on and thinking about my to-do lists. I even had (what I used to call) *workmares* in my sleep, half-lucid dreams riddled with anxiety about all the details I might have missed for a client or an event.

I was always traveling, consuming, partying, and burning the candle at both ends! It was not a conducive career for a family, or a romantic relationship, really. I dated mostly "mixologists," a.k.a. bartenders and nightcrawlers, the people who "got it" because they, too, were "in it." No balance. No off switch. I convinced myself that I *loved* my job and continued to do so for nearly a decade. The fast pace, being in a different space every day, traveling to places like Champagne, France, and Napa Valley, California, literally getting paid to taste the wine (and champagne) we would source for our accounts and events. Or attending the world's largest beverage alcohol conference in New Orleans, as a speaker. Or training Jamaican bartenders how to batch mai tais and classic rum punch for their new five-star chain hotel bars in Montego Bay. Or speaking to 300 individuals about the history of gin at a symposium in the UK by day and "researching" mixology culture (basically bar crawling) around London by night. It was fun, sure, really fun, but again, I longed for more and knew if I kept going at that pace, I wouldn't be alive to tell the tale.

I might have never left that career, a strange reflection to look upon now. My skills in convincing myself of something were quite persuasive back then. I was lined up for a big promotion and primed to one day take over the company. My salary was great on paper but when you actually looked at the math—time exchanged for money—I was averaging about $10 p/hour. No thanks. Soon after my realization that "perpetual party girl" was not a legacy I wanted to own, I started exploring my options.

I was sick of the party scene and had just exited an extremely toxic relationship with a man who, while we were living together for three years, had a double life and secret girlfriend for at least half of that time. He, too, was in the industry, which of course somehow justified his absence most nights until 3:00 a.m. and sometimes entire weekends with no contact; it made perfect sense. *How dare I be so accusatory and jealous? I was obviously the crazy one for not trusting him.* **That** right there is how I felt for a long time. A robot. Crazy. Exhausted. Spiraling. Sick. All signs of ignoring my gut, my soul nudges. I'd drink the abundant supply of booze I had access to at my fingertips to numb my screaming intuition. Then I'd drink more to try and sleep and quell the workmares and panic attacks. I'd distract myself with fifteen-hour shifts, hungover, handling cocktails and liquor bottles, so needless to say, "hair of the dog" was my motto during this sad and painful time in my life.

Rock bottom looks different for everybody. This perhaps wasn't *bottom*, but I sure did feel the weight of a boulder on my shoulders, knowing that if something didn't give, and soon, I'd be crushed. I moved out of the condo "we" owned (my secret life ex-boyfriend). I borrowed my busy lawyer friend's "den" (which was really a half wall indent, in the corner of her condo), and decked it out with a twin-sized air mattress. I set boundaries at work, took a pay cut, and hired an assistant to do the "heavy lifting" so I could take a step back. I wish I could say I took a radical turn with my health and sobriety, but this wasn't the case, not yet. Days turned into weeks, into months. I was developing back problems from sleeping on the air mattress for so long. My friend thought it was time, time for me to get off my ass and into a life that served me. She set up an online dating profile for me, much against my wishes. To satisfy her efforts and show gratitude for her hospitality, I humored her and started chatting with a few humans.

I had never dated this way before. I was a serial monogamist my entire dating life. Since I was thirteen years old, I had only long relationships; my shortest relationship was a year and a half long. The interesting thing about online dating is the algorithms. This was not a "swipe right to see my six pack" kind of site. Or a "hey girl" at some dingy bar. My friend set me up with the cream of the crop of dating sites, one of the expensive ones only serious people looking for partners, not hookups, go to.

First, there was the pilot. Blond hair, blue eyes, handsome, fit, no kids (and did I say pilot, hello!) and totally free of all partying and alcohol. Perfect on paper, polite and gentlemanly, but after one drink-free dinner, I knew the chemistry wasn't there. Next there was the corporate finance guy. Tall, dark, and handsome, super fit, no kids. Loved to party but in a "classy dinner party at his beautiful condo" kind of way, not the "wasted every night, affair-having way" I was used to. He was totally my type in a million ways, and the chemistry was definitely there.

Next suitor up was the restaurateur/designer/entrepreneur.

Ridiculously handsome, in a genuine and unpretentious way, no chiseled abs or cheesy haircut, he was rugged and mysterious. Messy divorce, a five-year-old son, lots of baggage, but . . . the chemistry. This was the chemistry they talk about in movies, a neurotransmitter boost you crave for days after it's gone. We chatted over the phone for a few days before deciding to meet up for dinner. We realized in one of our *get to know you* conversations, that, in fact, we already "knew" each other. Maybe I should have thought it to be a red flag that he used an alias on his dating profile, but I found it rather intriguing. We had met over a decade ago. I had had a total crush on some hunky bar owner my girlfriend (his roommate from university) had introduced me to. Our stars hadn't aligned for us then. He was married at the time, and I was too young, still in the peak of my twenties. Now, though, he was a divorced, single dad looking for real love. I knew after three days of chatting on the phone, one in-person pint of Guinness, and a rare steak at one of my favorite restaurants later, that he was my person.

His drama definitely got in the way for a while, months actually. Admittedly, he was afraid of his feelings; he needed to be sure before he invited someone into his bubble. He pushed me away—it could have been my job, my reputation, or a combo deal—but he wasn't ready for me to meet his son. So, I dated Mr. Corporate Finance for a few months. I was lucky to be distracted by his rooftop swimming pool, weekly dinner parties, and the fact that his condo was an elevator ride and about a hundred steps for me to get to work. It, like all things in my world, was fun but rather empty. I was still chatting casually to Mr. Restaurant because the magnetism we shared was undeniable. After about four months of settling for something that was fun but out of alignment, I broke up with the corporate finance guy, as it wasn't fair to either of us. In his mind, things were getting serious; in mine, he was merely a placeholder.

I found my own place. It was close to work and had a gym and a beautiful library, and it was clean and new. I moved my own bed in, queen-sized, that I had been storing at my parents' house. I stopped feeling sorry for myself and faced my deeply rooted fear of being on my own. I didn't go on another date and took down my dating profile. I started dating myself. I cooked beautiful meals for one and bought fresh-cut flowers for MY kitchen island. I spent my money on furniture, bedding with a thread count that made me feel luxurious, and art for my freshly painted walls rather than on mood enhancers and rounds of drinks at the bar.

I decided I was in a healthy enough place to go visit my best friends in Bermuda. Visiting them was always so healing and expansive for me. They live there as expatriates, but Lily was my roommate for many years prior to her moving. She knows me, probably better than I know myself sometimes. While she was happy for my singledom and new-found self-love, she also knew I would have regrets if I simply let Mr. Restaurateur just fade out. I had a choice, a fork in the road. I could follow the logic of my brain and weigh out the pros and cons. *He's divorced. He has a son. He owns several restaurants. He's ten years older than I am.* Or I could follow my gut, my intuition, the whisper in my soul telling me that he was my person.

I landed back in Toronto and texted him from the tarmac: "I need to see you." Apparently, he had been feeling the same way. Within six months, we moved in together. I became "Mom" to his son, our son. Within a year from that time, we were pregnant. I quit my job and ultimately my career in beverage alcohol. I started my own business in network marketing. Hubs had an excellent income, but I never wanted to fall back into the *we* trap, so I wanted a way to contribute to the household. I loved being in the NWM industry. I felt seen. I spent so many years playing drinking games with *the boys* that NWM felt empowering and rewarding. I didn't have to give up the things I loved about my previous career—leadership, team building, traveling, and teaching. I was now able to do those things my way. No boss. I worked when I wanted and some days not at all, and I was able to earn trips and attend global conferences, all with babies and pregnant bellies in tow. It freed up time and space to do the things I had missed while living in an alcohol-drenched cloud that was my previous life. I started writing again, exercising, and going for walks with friends.

Two babies later, Hubs and I really started feeling the nudge to get out of the hustle and bustle of city life. We desired land, space for our boys to grow and play, nature to roam in, fresh air to breathe, a garden to grow, and new adventures to experience. Real estate prices in the city were becoming completely unaffordable. So, the search began. We put a couple of offers in on small rural homes and got squeezed out, once by a bidding war and next by a home design television show. We considered moving to our cottage, but it's on an island and would be too much of a commute to get around. We searched high and low for almost a year.

Just for fun one day, Hubs was looking on MLS at agricultural properties. *Yeah, like we are farmers, ha!* He found one that looked interesting. No photos of any house or outbuildings, only property, but the property was magical. Seventy acres of protected forest and farm fields. Magical, but also intimidating, much like how our soul whispers often are. How would we, two citiots, take care of seventy acres of forest? My brain said no. *This is ridiculous, we need a house, we can't build something, we need to be close to schools and shops and hospitals.* Then that whisper showed up again: *But what if this is it, your forever home?* We decided we had nothing to lose and went to check it out.

The realtor for the property was away on holiday but arranged for us to meet the man who owned it. He reminded me of a character from a Wild West film. Leather jacket, open buttons at the top, cowboy hat and boots, cigarette hanging out of his mouth, and an accent that sang like a southern drawl even though he was from rural Ontario. We followed his modest pickup truck down a little dirt road, questioning our choice to be alone in the woods with this cowboy-esque stranger. To the best of our knowledge from viewing it on Google Earth, this property was mostly forest with what looked like a garage and a barn. We drove for about a mile and stopped. There was a house, a really cute bungalow with cedar shingles and a sweet little porch.

We later discovered that the property was zoned as agriculture because they were expecting farmers to come in and tear down the buildings to farm the land. We instantly fell in love. It wasn't an easy feat. Mortgaging a farm is a very different process than mortgaging a typical home. We jumped through all the hoops because we refused to lose this one, not this time. We landed our dream home, a farm in a magical, wild, and picture-perfect forest. In a logical world, we wouldn't have ever qualified for the place because of a myriad of reasons I won't delve into here. Yet in a world where our desires lead the way, logic has no place in it. There is simply our soul's calling, the magnetic pull toward our visions. And to get there, it means we need to do it scared, do it messy, and lean into the liminal spaces that exist. Every single time I have listened to my intuition, it has always shown me a way forward, a solution, a magical opening and beginning. The citiots learned to farm, harvest their crops, raise more than thirty farm animals along with their three boys, all while juggling homeschooling (during the pandemic) and growing two successful businesses.

Has the journey to get here been easy? No. Has it been worth it?

Absolutely. My vision now is to build a legacy, generational impact and wealth, and that happens when we stop chasing the details and start holding the vision and leaning into our intuition. The details work themselves out, as they always will, once you have made a decision. You have the power to **choose your own adventure**, at least the things you have control over. You have the ability to allow a single whisper to change the trajectory of your whole life. *Are you listening? Are you willing to surrender and lean into her guidance?* Your whispers are your soul's river. Start flowing with it and ditch the upstream swim. Trust the direction; even if there's an undercurrent or a patch of stagnancy, your river will always lead you home. As long as you listen and trust those nudges, and whispers, you will always end up exactly where you are meant to be.

SECTION 2

KATE WARREN
KYLIE WAECHTER
MICHELLE RILLI
JESSICA JOHNSTONE

Sometimes you are so focused on one thing that you are almost blind-sided by all the things you didn't even see coming.

There are few things that change you as much as motherhood does—the journey starts from the very moment you consider having children, and becoming a mother isn't an easy road for everyone. Whatever you experience on your path to motherhood, things change and you are never really the same. No one tells you that your child's birth shifts you from the person you knew to someone you will need to discover. It isn't just about fewer fancy nights out or needing a bigger vehicle. The change we are referring to is how you see yourself and the invisible pressures that come along with motherhood. It is often messy, confusing, and full of ups and downs, but eventually—although no one's timeline is the same—you find your unique flow and evolve and embrace this beautiful new person you have become. You begin to connect to who you are and your understanding of what's important and what you hold dear. It all happens on a level you didn't know was possible. This instinctual connection can be so deep and fast that it overwhelms us. Some describe it as creating distrust, confusion, a fog, anxiety, sadness, or a whole host of other emotions of an intensity you didn't know was possible. It is in these initial transitions to motherhood that we often drown out the sounds of our intuition, making the whispers harder to hear.

But the fog does lift. The reality that your heart is now living outside of your physical body starts to enhance your gut feelings and many feel they grow more in tune with their intuition. In society today, there is also a lot of distraction that can make you question yourself. *Hmm, to trust your inner knowing or follow the latest trends.* It's a challenge at the beginning as there is a lot of information and well-meaning yet unsolicited advice and opinions coming at you. This can lead to a seemingly huge space between what people tell you and what you feel in your soul when it comes to your role as a mother and you as an autonomous person.

These stories share the messy parts and the awakenings—the moments that allow for a reconnection with your heart and the shifts that help you stop overthinking and shed what no longer serves you so you can reconnect to your truth. They bring us hope that when we focus on connecting to what matters to us, the change can move us toward a more authentic and aligned life.

Waking up from the fog of early motherhood is not easy. For some, they will realize that they are exactly where they want to be on their journey. For others, the discomfort will require a major shift. But then again, maybe this is the moment they have been waiting for to really lean into what they want out of life. These amazing little humans we get to raise become our greatest teachers; they allow us to stretch in new ways and remind us to move toward our biggest dreams and hearts' desires.

Make powerful waves, big, bold moves, and listen to the whispers of your wild soul.

Chapter 6

PIECES OF ME

KATE WARREN

If we aren't willing to lead ourselves to growth directly, the Universe steps in and ushers us toward it instead.

@warren__kate

Kate Warren

Kate Warren is a multi-passionate creative, entrepreneur, business owner times two, daughter, sister, mother, wife, and now an author! What the heck?! This is so cool! An entrepreneur at heart, Kate has always desired to do life at her own pace. She enjoys helping others by sharing her own experiences, healing, and vision. Kate is on a mission to empower women by helping them own who are they unapologetically and step into themselves wholeheartedly.

Although she has two distinct businesses—photography and mentorship—the common theme is empowerment. Kate's ultimate desire is for people to feel seen and heard. Her other brand, *Keep Them Wild*, was birthed as a result of navigating challenges within motherhood. It's easy to feel lost in motherhood, which further ripples into who we are as women. But we don't have to do it alone. Kate's communities are built for deep soulful connection, empowerment, and a sustainable lifestyle. Connect with her— say hello! Connection is the cornerstone to both her businesses and is vital for support during these seasons of motherhood + womanhood.

IG: @WARREN__KATE

Josh + Nora—you two are constantly giving me the strength and space to evolve, expand, and discover who I am.

You either walk inside your story and own it, or you stand outside your story and hustle for your worthiness.

—Brené Brown, *Rising Strong*

This was more than a move to a small town, this was about trusting my intuition and trusting myself to take the lead in my own life. I've always been someone who takes advantage of opportunities when they present themselves. Someone who adapts, forges her own path, and seeks a different way of being when things no longer work. I've always been a big dreamer. When my husband and I started dating in 2013, we would go on long road trips, and it was in those car rides when we would dream together. We would talk about where we wanted to travel, what kind of life we wanted to create, what kind of animals we wanted to rescue, what direction we wanted to go for work, among so many other things. Those car rides were where we took advantage of uninterrupted time together. And in that time together, we dreamed our dreams and set the intention to make them our reality. Those car rides were our vision board manifesting in our hearts, our minds. Determined to make it happen while leaning into the sweet surrender that we would always be supported as long as we were willing to go first, take chances, bet on ourselves and each other, and never give up on each other or our vision. Those car rides were where we envisioned moving to a small town (with forests and trails for hiking), developing a close-knit bond with our community, and raising our future children away from the hustle and bustle of the city.

At the time of writing this chapter, I am leaving a lifestyle I am used to, one that I have known my whole life, for something I've never had. But I think this is the point—to evolve and outgrow things that were once familiar to us so we can step into deeper alignment. And sometimes, if we aren't willing to lead ourselves to growth directly, the Universe steps in and ushers us toward it instead. You see, my relationship with my husband is the most stable, safe, and solid relationship I have had in my life. However, every relationship experiences situations that rock you and your relationship. While in the eye of the storm, you have no idea how you'll pull through until you're actually on the other side. Once you make it through, you realize you wouldn't be who you are and where you are without going through that experience. That's what happened to us. There was a series of big things and little things that slowly happened over a year and a half that led me to take a serious look at my life. To re-evaluate my priorities, identify what was important to me, and confront the areas I was neglecting. It was a year that forced me to discover what would make me happy again. The truth is that I wasn't truly happy when I had this aha moment. The truth is that when I became a mother (spring 2018), my whole world changed. I know this resonates with many people. But the problem was, I went about my life as if I just didn't have a baby. I experienced many challenges very early on when I became a mother: not really being able to breastfeed, a lack of sleep, postpartum mood and anxiety disorder (PPMAD), transitioning into this new role, figuring out who I was as a mother, and learning how to navigate being a parent with my husband (who was also dealing with his own challenges that came with being a new father). I felt completely lost. Alone. I felt like I was constantly being judged by others (oh hello, anxiety, I see you now). I had stopped dreaming. I couldn't remember the last time I felt more . . . me. The only thing I could control, the only thing I could distract myself with, the only place where I felt worthy and knew I was good at was my work. As a photographer, I was able to choose when I went back to work. At the peak of my sleep deprivation, lack of confidence, and struggling marriage, I consciously chose to start working. The more lost I felt, the more anxious I became, the more I worked. The cycle continued. The year my daughter was born was my best year in business to date. But none of that mattered. It didn't matter because I wasn't happy. I was barely sleeping, my marriage was not in a great place, my mental health tanked, and my physical health was a reflection of all of it. I had little to no energy. My life felt lackluster, dull, routine. *Is this what motherhood was?* I wasn't spending the quality time with my daughter that I had imagined I would. No one knew that I was feeling this way. No one knew this because I didn't even recognize it at the time. I remember the night that literally changed it all. It was the second winter (January 2020) with our daughter; she was a year and a half old. I was folding laundry after spending over an hour getting my daughter down for bed, my husband was working out in the basement where I was, and I just started crying uncontrollably. I put down the clothes and said, "Babe, I don't think I am okay." That same night I made an appointment with a therapist. That night I decided to reclaim my power, to dig deeper and get to the root as to why I was feeling the way that I was. Healing is hard. Like it's so fucking hard. It's scary as hell. And being vulnerable is un-freaking-comfortable.

It ended up with me spending 2020 in its entirety dedicating myself to healing. To forgive. To live with purpose and passion, with love for my family. By working on myself, I changed. Bit by bit. I began to see glimpses of the girl I once used to be and began feeling the intensity of the woman I was becoming. And I was happier. Despite feeling notice-ably happier than before, I still felt like something was missing. Like I didn't belong here. I knew something needed to change but couldn't quite figure it out. I was in the middle of my inner healing (which, by the way, is a lifelong journey), and I was evolving as a mother, a wife, a business owner, and most importantly, as a woman. The year 2020 was when I outgrew where I was living. January 2021, during one of my daughter's naps, my husband came upstairs and just looked at me and asked the question he had asked me one too many times before: "What if we moved to a small town?" Though he had asked me this many times before, it never felt right. He grew up in a small town, and I am from one of the biggest cities in Ontario. City life is all I have ever known. To me, small towns are places you visit when you want a weekend escape. Live there permanently? I don't know that I had this dying urge to do so previously, though we had envisioned it at some point. This time, however, it felt different. I looked at him and said, "I actually don't hate that idea." It's hard to explain this feeling, it just felt right. For me, for us, for our daughter. Or perhaps it was all the *Schitt's Creek* episodes I binged on that were doing the talking for me. Whatever the reason behind this urge, it was there. And I needed to see it through.

During this period of healing, I learned to pay attention to my intui-tion. That whisper that is forever urging me and nudging me toward my dreams, even when they make absolutely no sense to me or anyone around me. And when my husband asked me that question, my gut was screaming a big fucking YES. Within four months, we found the most perfect town for us. We sold our house in the city and bought our dream house in a small town. The stars felt like they were aligning. In four months, our lives completely changed. I decided to leave a life that I was comfortable with to live somewhere that I knew nothing about. But that whisper needed to be heard. And once I listened to her, I started to feel like myself again. It took me to experience severe burnout, to crash and break into a million little pieces to get my health—emotional, mental, and physical—back on track. To make my happiness a priority, to get my marriage back on track, to realize the lifestyle we were living wasn't actually what I wanted, like I once thought I did. As it turns out, I wasn't all that happy. I mean, I was okay but not happy. I know this because I had stopped dreaming. It felt like the light within me continued to flicker on and off, clinging obsessively to anything that remotely made me feel alive. I continued to find my escape such as work, which felt great while I was in the moment. However, I still wasn't dreaming. All of this started to dawn on me late winter 2020. I took a long, hard look at my current life and realized I wasn't actually happy, fulfilled, or nourished. Let me tell you, that is a hard thing to acknowledge. From the outside my life seemed great; I had a new and healthy baby girl, an incredible husband, a warm house to come home to, and a thriving business, but I was no longer the person I was before I gave birth to the most perfect baby girl. Still, despite experiencing the lowest lows, I wouldn't change that year and a half for anything. It nearly broke me; I felt disconnected from my body and soul. I was ungrounded. I didn't realize I was in a perpetual war with myself.

When March 2020 hit the scene, I didn't work for four months. At first, anxiety wrapped herself around me like a familiar blanket. I had nowhere to hide. I had no option but to sit with all the emotions that had been surfacing. I couldn't bury myself in work to regain a sense of control instead of spiraling away. At first, it was hard to function at a slower pace. An intentional pace. After a month, I started to really enjoy this slow-paced life at home. I spent more quality time with my almost two-year-old daughter. My husband was working from home and we had each other's presence at all times, even if we were doing our own thing at home. I felt more at peace with myself. I rested, I picked up like a million new hobbies and fell back into an old true passion of mine: helping young children feel comfortable, seen, and heard. As someone who also has a degree in psychology focusing on infant and child development, I found myself enrolling in classes and courses in this area. Slowly but surely, pieces of me started to come back. For those four months that I was off work, I felt like I finally had that maternity leave that I had never allowed myself to have. I was ungrounded. Unaligned. I was sleepwalking through my life. I was anxious, dressed up in being a successful business owner, being that superhero mom. I was living up these titles, these labels people were giving me at the expense of my health, my wellness, my relationships with my family. It took me to this point to wake up. Internally, I was at a breaking point, but it was hard to recognize because it was disguised as something else. Navigating through such a massive transition that motherhood is, is sticky. As women, we are often struggling through it alone because no one is talking about this evolution from maiden to motherhood to womanhood. There is virtually no support, no community, no nothing. Even though I felt incredibly alone during this season, I know I wasn't the only one. It was only when I started to share my experience (my own version of healing) that I knew this was something that needed to be talked about. We are mourning who we used to be while evolving into someone new. This is not easy. Losing a sense of who you are while taking on arguably the most challenging, amazing, important role in the world, a parent, comes with its challenges. This loss of identity—not knowing who I was, neglecting myself to keep control over anything I could—woke me up. This is not who I wanted to be; it was ungrounding. It was messy. I felt like I was walking through the motions of life. I wanted motherhood to be better than that. There are so many pieces to me, as there are to you. We often label ourselves, label who other people are to one thing, don't we? Humans are not that simple. We are complex beings. There is more to us than motherhood, but it's a big part of who we are. So, how do we mesh all parts of ourselves together? Well, I am still figuring that out. But this time I am riding the waves and seasons of motherhood and womanhood more grounded. Feeling aligned and supported.

Chapter 7

BREAKING FREE

KYLIE WAECHTER

Hold onto the ones
who stand by you,
show up for you,
and support you,
no matter what.

@kyliewaechter

Kylie Waechter

Kylie Waechter is a new author who loves connecting with women who share a similar fierceness and joy for conscious living. She is committed to her own personal growth, learning and unlearning, and she is raising a family intuitively, not how society says she should. Her ability to create her own path and live unconventionally is an inspiration to young mothers. Kylie is a proud wife to a man who can fix anything and mother to a strong-willed and sweet boy plus (biggest surprise of 2021!) twins who are on the way as she wrote her chapter in *Whisper*. Kylie is a true creative spirit and leans into her passions, which include design, photography, reading, baking, exploring nature, essential oils, and spending time with her family. She loves curling up with a great suspense novel by Shari Lapena or Lisa Jewell. Kylie is hoping that her story inspires other women to listen to the whispers of their hearts and looks forward to connecting with her readers.

IG: @KYLIEWAECHTER

To my children, know that everything I do is for a bright and happy future for you. And to women everywhere, follow your heart, as it will lead you in the right direction.

Happiness comes from living as you need to, as you want to. As your inner voice tells you to. Happiness comes from being who you actually are instead of who you think you are supposed to be.

—Shonda Rhimes, *Year of Yes*

I like to think of myself as someone who has always gone after what I want. I have always been someone who takes chances, trusts their intuition, chases their dreams, and goes after their goals.

When my husband and I first met, we soon discovered that we both shared a great love for the western provinces in Canada, specifically Alberta. We often talked about staying open to moving there should an opportunity present itself to us. We would visualize what our life would be like in the Rockies, breathing in mountain air, living at a slower pace, enjoying hikes in Banff, kicking back at the Calgary Stampede. Yes, our lives would change drastically.

The conversations would come and go. But it was always on our minds; even when we found out we were having a baby, through all our moves, an engagement and a wedding, Alberta, Canada, was always there. Much like that headache that never goes away even though you take a pill to alleviate it, the dull ache is always there. That was how I felt. I always had this whisper telling me, *Kylie, this is not your full potential; this is not where home is.*

I was always taught to trust the intuition we are given as women. We were given it for a reason. My intuition would become my guiding light the moment I became a mother in 2018. Motherhood is the best gift I have ever received. Holding that precious baby boy in my arms was a dream that I have had my whole life. Being a mother is what I am meant to do. I remember sitting in that hospital room holding his little hand, promising him that his daddy and mommy would give him everything he deserved and more. From that moment on, our lives changed. Many things that we allowed to hold space in our lives started to dissolve. Misaligned friendships fell apart in the most natural way, and our dreams became bigger and went from traveling the world to providing a loving, honest household where we never had to fake being happy and where we had financial freedom.

Amid getting engaged, planning a wedding, and getting immersed into motherhood, moving provinces, or even traveling to Western Canada, got put on the backburner. I knew it would happen when it was meant to, and not one second sooner. Timing is everything, and forcing the timing of things has never been my style. I believe things happen when they are supposed to—stressing out about it or worrying will not speed up Divine timing. Christmas 2020 is when everything changed for us.

My mom and stepdad, who live in British Columbia, were spending Christmas with us and dropped the news that they were moving back to Ontario to be closer to us. Exciting, right? Especially since I had not lived close to them in six years. I shared the news with my partner, who was happy for me, as he knew just how much I had been wanting to live close to them, especially since I entered motherhood. Throughout the next two months, my husband would say things like "Is moving to Calgary off the table?" or "Do you think we should still think about moving out there?" Every time he asked me those questions, my stomach did a flip, that intuition kicked in, the whisper still spoke, ever so softly but firmly. I knew that we had to consider this move; I needed to have this conversation with my mom.

When I shared with my mom that our hearts were urging us to move to Alberta, even though they had just announced their move to Ontario, she was overjoyed! I had not wanted to wreck her plan, and it went better than I ever expected. After explaining to her our thoughts and where our heads were, she said something along the lines of "Well, that is actually really great news because us moving to Ontario does not seem to be lining up, and there are a lot of roadblocks." Hearing her say that was a sigh of relief! Right then, we decided that we would move forward with our move to Alberta. We knew with certainty that this move was right for us all along. The lifestyle, the opportunities, and the fresh start we were craving were becoming closer than ever.

The next three months were very emotional for us. We decided to not tell anyone our news until everything was in place and finalized. Growing up, I was always told by my mom to keep my next move in life a secret so no one could give me unnecessary advice. I am so thankful for that life lesson from my mom. Sure enough, things fell into place, my husband got an amazing job, and my passion for photography was like a fire underneath me.

We established the dates for when my husband would start work, and it was only at that point that we shared our news with everyone. There was a lot to do but also a lot of emotions that came up, and we were leaving in just under two months. People were sad, there were tears, and we both experienced a lot of guilt for moving away from family in Ontario. We had built up a tight community and were close to extended family who adore our son so much. However, the whisper continued to show herself, firm, fierce, and clear as day. *Kylie, this is what is best for you and your family. This move will be incredible.* If you're nodding your head because there have been moments in your life where you've given into the pressure of maintaining status quo and suppressing your desires, here is what I will share with you: **In the end, only you know what is best for you and your family. When you become a parent, your perspective on life shifts immensely. The only thing that matters is providing an amazing life for yourself and your children.** Taking care of them is top priority and doing that somewhere where we always felt stuck or where we could never get ahead is not what we wanted or even what others wanted for us. Our friends and family understood our decision and supported us. We treasured the next few months we spent with them.

The weeks leading up to any life transitions are always chaotic with emotions running on an all-time high. They are also, of course, bitter-sweet. You never quite know how time flies by. Something else I realized during these weeks leading up to our move was that we held high expectations from people in our lives. I remember sitting in the living room with my glass of white wine after our son fell asleep. My husband, Steve, was cleaning up in the kitchen and I blurted out loud, "I am really hurt and disappointed; I feel like some people really don't care that we are leaving." Steve, nodding in agreement, said, "I know, babe, I feel the same way; hopefully things change soon." I called my mom the next day and shared with her how I felt. She shared with me that when she made the move from Ontario to Florida, she went through the same thing.

She was disappointed in how some people acted and was surprised at how the ones she didn't have a strong relationship with really made an effort instead. And today, those are the friendships that are strongest in her world. There was a bittersweet whisper that continued to echo with this transition: *Kylie, it's okay; they are not your people. Not your soul people, at least.* I was living under a shell until this point with my own expectations and assumptions. I thought that because we had been friends for several years that nothing would change. But that in itself is a fallacy. Of course, things would change. We evolve every single day, every single moment. And now that I am moving more than 2,000 miles away, things would shift even more. Something one of my very best friends shared with me when I opened up to her about my feelings stuck with me: "Having long-distance friends is really amazing, as your time spent together becomes more intentional and meaningful." For some reason, I felt that. The whisper nodded affirmatively too. It gave me perspective and helped me regain confidence in my friendships. I know now my friendships will inevitably change. I am not there to go shopping or have coffee dates anymore. Now we will have week-long visits and deeper connections whenever we visit each other or hop on a video call. Our conversations will be intentional, and our text messages and how we show up for each other will be intentional as well—more than they were before and that is something that I am looking forward to. Having my friends visit and seeing our new life is something that makes me very excited. Going through major life changes really teaches you who your people are. Hold onto the ones who stand by you, show up for you, and support you, no matter what.

Moving your family and uprooting the life you once knew to chase a life that feels more expansive, freeing, and light isn't a walk in the park. There were far too many moments when I felt like I was losing my mind.

But I was determined to sink into this feeling of openness, freedom, and weightlessness both my family and me. I was determined to start a simpler life out there. Less is more, I firmly believed that. Less things = less chaos and a clearer mind. Having a lot of material things in your home causes chaos in your mind. Decluttering our lives figuratively and literally will give us a clearer outlook on life and a good fresh start in our new lives. Release old, stagnant friendships, relationships, and opportunities that no longer align or serve you mutually. Declutter your social media feeds, your contact list, your commitments, and yes, even those pesky $27 subscriptions you barely use. This is not to say that packing up a home and deciding what is important enough to keep versus what to part with wasn't hard. It was emotionally draining, especially being a mom. Going through our son's baby clothes, the items we as a family collected over the last eight years of being married and now a growing family—deciding what meant more to me than others or what we should sell or bring with us—all of it bittersweet, exhausting, and overwhelming. I'd do that all day and spend time with friends and family in the evenings. It felt like I was not even in my own body anymore. But I knew that I had to get everything done by a certain date.

The day came when the final goodbyes were said. Emotions were high. Part of me just wanted to get it over with because I had been dreading these goodbyes for months, to the point where it made me physically ill. The other part of me never wanted these moments to end. Holding onto our loved ones and hugging them with tears streaming down our faces, these were our people, the ones who have helped us through so much, who have never left our side. After buckling our son in the car, we hugged one last time before starting our car and driving off. One last honk of the horn before we drove around the corner. Our adventure had begun. It was time to feel all the emotions and to make this a positive family trip. Something we would always remember. A trip that we could tell our son all about one day, and how he was a massive part of this move.

THE CALGARY DIARIES

Day 1:

Nothing prepares you for the feeling of leaving somewhere you feel like you don't belong. The only word that comes to my mind is freedom. Sitting in the passenger's seat with tears streaming down my face as my husband drove and our son was in the backseat, I turned to him and said, "I can't believe that we are doing this. We are finally creating the life that we have dreamed and talked about." He looked at me, smiled, squeezed my hand and said, "I know, babe, I can't wait to see what we accomplish."

We had no idea what to expect as we started our road trip, especially with a three-year-old. We drove about six and a half hours that day. Going into this road trip, the last thing I wanted to do was too much planning. Over the last two years, I felt like all we did was plan, plan, and plan—first with our wedding and then with this move. When it came to the road trip, we agreed that we wouldn't make too many plans.

We decided that we would drive until we were tired and look to see what city we were in or close to and stop there for the night. We drove from Barrie, Ontario, to Sault Ste Marie that day. We arrived at our hotel, excited and exhausted! One day down, four more to go!

Day 2:

We woke up bright-eyed and excited, full of energy! We had a quick breakfast and packed up our truck and trailer, excited to drive seven and a half hours to Thunder Bay! Our last full day in Ontario, or so we thought.

Not long after we got on the road, we heard a noise after we went over a pothole. We didn't think much of it. Two minutes later, we had someone speed up beside us, honking their horn. As we rolled down our windows, we heard "You are going to lose a tire!" We pulled onto a side street, in the rain, and noticed that one of the tires from the trailer was emitting smoke and making a noise that did not sound comforting. We sat on the side of the road, trying to call up different car mechanics, hoping that someone would be available to fix it on a Saturday. This went on for about thirty minutes, until we found a place that could help us, but not until Monday morning. With it being a Saturday, our choices were nonexistent. So there we were, excited to start our second day, only to find ourselves staying in the same hotel we had stayed in the night before.

Initially, we felt angry and frustrated. Our first thoughts were: *We are wasting so much extra money staying at hotels for an extra two nights* and *What a waste of time this weekend will be.* We quickly snapped out of it and shifted our perspective to one of growth and optimism. I heard the whisper calmly reassuring me, *Kylie, for whatever reason, you are not meant to be driving this weekend. You are meant to stay put and have this extra quality time together as a family to relax and enjoy each other's company.* We did exactly that! We had a pizza party in our hotel room, went swimming as a family, and for the first time in a really long time, we felt like we could actually relax without feeling like we had to be doing something else.

Day 3:

You never really know what you need until it slaps you in the face. For us, it was the day we found ourselves stuck in Sault Ste Marie. The Universe, God, or whatever higher power you believe in was definitely looking out for us, giving us the weekend to sit back and spend quality time together. Going to bed that night, we felt calm, well rested, and ready to get back on the road. Michael, our son, thrived all day having us all to himself with no other distractions. What a happy and funny kid we have! I couldn't feel any prouder of our family and the decisions we made.

Day 4:

Wow, what a beautiful drive! Driving through the mountains, as Michael was sleeping in the back, holding hands with my sweetie and just enjoying the peacefulness and how content we both felt is a feeling I'll never forget. We felt free again. Calgary was getting closer with every minute. This is where our lives would change for the better. I felt it. We settled into an adorable family-run motel for the night so that we were ready for the long day ahead of us.

Day 5:

I definitely felt different when I woke up. A sense of relief, excitement, and nervousness was coursing through me. As relieved as I was that this journey was almost coming to a close, I knew yet another one was about to begin. In about seven hours, we would be in our new home, unloading and unpacking, making it a safe place for us and a welcoming place for friends and family. I found myself looking at the clock more frequently and getting more restless by the hour. Finally, we were five minutes from the house and my nerves were strong at this point, my stomach full of fluttering butterflies. Pulling up to the house, I almost cried out of happiness. From all the plans and emotions from the past year, this is what it has come to: us finally walking into a home that would be the best stepping-stone for our family. I couldn't believe this was actually happening. Walking up the stairs and stepping into our home for the first time, I felt peace. The whisper echoed it too. *Here is where you belong. Here is where you are free to bloom and grow.* I felt peaceful for the first time in the last two years after planning each step, spending as much time as we could with loved ones before we left, sifting through each and every belonging we owned—asking ourselves whether it was important enough to come across the country with us—selling all our furniture, and living out of suitcases for a couple weeks. Peace was a beautiful feeling to come home to. Yes, we were home indeed.

I remember feeling immense loads of guilt as soon as we decided we were doing this thing after all. Guilt over leaving my family and friends. Guilt over taking Michael away from the only people he knew. Guilt over moving away from our support system. We all know just how challenging it can be to make new friends as an adult, or *was that a story I was telling myself?* the whisper retorted back lovingly. How on earth did one make friends anymore? Would Michael forget his friends and family back in Ontario that he had grown to know and love the past three years? I remember feeling so anxious about everything leading up to our move, yet deep within, my whisper kept telling me, *It will all work out for you, you'll see.*

When my best friend told me that long-distance friendships are truly amazing, she wasn't lying. I felt relieved to hear that—to know that I could always lean on my support system, no matter how many miles were between us. We've been in Calgary for just over a month now, and she couldn't have been more correct! My conversations with loved ones are more meaningful. Although I am counting down the days until they visit us, I cherish our video calls and always look forward to the next one! My lesson here has been that it is up to us to create and cultivate the energy within the relationships we desire. It is up to us to show up fully, with intention.

I feel lighter. I no longer feel this heavy cloud of anxiety over me. I feel free here. Michael is happier, and he loves his new home and all the fun new things to do. Being a kid is supposed to be so much fun, full of laughter and being free. Our home is lighter and brighter, and so is our future. Our life as a family feels expansive, one rooted in love and freedom and that tunes into our internal compass as much as possible. To hear the whispers that call our name. It hit me that our whispers will never lead us wrong. They are there for a reason, and it is up to us to honor them. When we were sharing with our friends and family about our decision to move across the country, I was surprised by just how many people told us that they wished that they could do what we were doing. That we were so brave, and they were jealous that they couldn't do the same. But to that question, I always asked, why not? And I ask you, who is reading this currently, why not you? You are not a tree; you can move! If you are unhappy with your situation, if you feel stuck in your job or within your relationships, you have the freedom to fix that. It might take some planning and a whole lot of courage, but you can do it. It doesn't have to be a 2,000+ miles, it could even be a few hours, because believe me, those few hours will put things into perspective for you. Like me, you, too, will feel a sense of freedom and peace.

Chapter 8

TAKING MY POWER BACK

MICHELLE RILLI

There's liberation in being raw, real, and unapologetic, and in removing those filters.

@rilli_me

Michelle Rilli

Michelle Rilli is a dedicated mom of two beautiful free spirits, a devoted wife to her husband, Rob, and a good friend to many. Often referred to as a "Jill of all traits," she is no stranger to wearing many hats and bringing people and teams together to achieve positive change and growth for her clients. Michelle started her career as an Engineering Technologist but pivoted to sales and marketing after realizing her true passion. She went back to school for Marketing Management and never looked back. She's an entrepreneur at heart who has been recognized as a problem solver while empowering the people around her. An avid explorer, always wandering but not usually lost. She enjoys planned spontaneity, structured chaos, and dancing like no one's watching, and she's never met a pinot noir she hasn't liked. This is her first experience as an author.

IG: @RILLI_ME

To my children, my rainbows after the storm, my purpose, my why, my everything. I hope to instill the same courage and strength in you that my parents have instilled in me.

To my husband, for always supporting me and for knowing that self-care also = girls' trips.

To my parents, who gave us the life they never had and for ingraining the values and integrity we lead with today.

To my mother-in-law, whose selflessness and courage knows no bounds. Thank you for raising an amazing husband and father and for helping us raise our children.

I'd rather regret the things I've done than regret the things I haven't done.
—Lucille Ball

It's a beautiful, sunny Monday morning. I'm sitting in my car half laughing and half crying, five months pregnant, jobless, ready to go back home and pack up my life. The moving trucks are booked, and the plans have been set. *I wanted this, so why am I so upset?*

Like a true Cancerian crab, I held on as hard and as long as I could. I gave it everything I had left to give. But like a crab, if you hold on for too long, something will snap that claw off. And when it did, I was equal parts relieved and lost. I took a long, deep breath and exhaled with an incredible release. Most of the anxiety and negative feelings just washed away, but then anger crept in. Yes, I wanted this, but it wasn't on my own terms. I had my power back, but I also lost it at the same time. By this time I was five months pregnant (and visibly showing) with no job prospects, as I'd intended to stay and push through until my maternity leave started in three months. Here's some truth for you: Looking for a new job while visibly pregnant is daunting. We've always been told not to disclose that we're pregnant, as it's none of their business. Do you want to work for a company that you lied to right from the beginning? Will they want you?

Will they keep you? Ultimately, I looked very pregnant by the time any interviews lined up, and I didn't find a new role. In the big picture, this was how I was meant to take control back and have a season that was just mine—a season dedicated to my growth, evolution, and power, although I didn't quite understand this yet.

Have you ever been in a new job and within a short time your gut is telling you to run? That "fight or flight" feeling kicks in and you feel trapped with doubt and fear falling all around you like heavy rain. Did you listen to your gut or ignore it? Did you listen to the whisper saying, "Red flag!" Or did you ignore it? I know I did, and likely, you have too. My gut was telling me that this was a bad decision, and this was not the job for me. My brain said, "You're a problem solver and you can fix things," so I went against my better judgment and ignored my gut, even though it was screaming at me. I thought by staying put I was in fact listening to my intuition; however, it was judgment and social obligations masquerading as intuition. I didn't realize just how much pressure we, as women, face on a daily basis. We try so hard to fit into the mold that has been designed for the patriarchy, and we inadvertently participate in it too.

After a traumatic birth and long recovery with my first child, I was desperate to feel "normal" again. My company had offered me a new role within the organization if I went back months early, and I jumped. From the outside, I was thriving. I had a healthy baby and a great job. I had my shit together, but this was far from the truth. The pressure to get back to work and be the perfect working mom is so strong. My body was still healing, and I hadn't even begun to process what had happened to me. After being on bedrest and unable to really enjoy my new family for weeks, I was faced with a long and painful recovery that lasted months. I felt robbed of my maternity leave, robbed of the perfect breastfeeding experience, and robbed of the memories I was supposed to be making. My Insta feed was full of picture-perfect families, and I felt an incredible pressure to pull myself up and move forward like all moms do. I was searching for something external because I didn't realize I was still recovering internally. When a new opportunity presented itself for more money and a bigger title, I jumped again. I put so much pressure on myself to bounce back, and I used the corporate ladder as my escape plan.

It took me a few years, full of postpartum anxiety and post-traumatic stress (PTSD), to even consider that I wasn't "okay." My husband wanted another child, and I was terrified. I couldn't even talk about it without breaking down. I had everything and was supposed to be happy, but I wanted to quit my job and run. I was dealing with the anxiety of reliving one of the hardest times of my life, while it was becoming more and more difficult to walk through my office doors every day. *Do you look for a new opportunity while trying to conceive? Or do you stay because the stress of searching and having a child soon after being hired would feel worse than staying put?* I ignored my gut again and stayed. What happened next was the catalyst for a major life change. We got pregnant, and although we were absolutely elated, the worry set in and I couldn't shake a feeling. My first baby was a rainbow baby and came after a miscarriage. I tried not to worry and did everything I could to remain calm and at peace for those early weeks, including yoga, eating well, and taking my vitamins. But being surrounded by so much toxic negativity at work while struggling to hold my values and integrity high resulted in increased anxiety, and it was starting to take its toll. A miscarriage came and then another followed. *Was this the reason I miscarried? Was it all my fault?* Up to 20 percent of women miscarry, so it's extremely common, but it's not commonly discussed, and we often end up blaming ourselves (and taking on the blame from others too).

It was time to take my power back. To take control of my future and make myself proud. I wasn't sure what I wanted at that time, but I was sure of what I didn't want. I didn't want to spend my weeks working sixty-plus hours every week in a toxic environment only to come home and not be present in my life, our life. And I was willing to do whatever it takes, even work a hundred hours every week, as long as it was in an environment that inspired me, fueled me, and challenged me to be better and do better, with purpose. Although we loved our home and city, what we thought was our forever home was temporary, and something continued to pull us west to the suburbs. We wanted to be closer to family, to have more space for the kids, and to build the future we desired. Our plans were set within that same month. We quietly sold our house and purchased our next one. Knowing that we were putting our family first and reclaiming control of our lives helped me step into #freedommindset right away. Knowing that *I*, not anyone else, held power over my time, my desires, and my life choices was all the certainty I needed. It was my sense of certainty. Not a job, not anyone else. I was ready to close this chapter and pivot my life. Being on this new path gave me a sense of innate peace and calm. We finally conceived and carried our second rainbow baby. I was cautiously optimistic, and when we came out of the "danger zone," we slowly started to share our baby plans. We finally had our rainbow after the storm, and I would stick it out at this job for a few more months until we moved. I'd often dreamed (like actual nightly dreams) about how I would quit a job I didn't like—*a cake, a singing telegram, a microphone drop proclaiming, "I quit!"* I could never be anything less than professional, but one can dream.

Moving during a pregnancy wasn't new to us, as this was our second time. Since I no longer had a job, I focused all my time on our move and renovation. I was too busy and tired to process what happened or worry about what was to come. Baby number two came, and she was perfect. We had a few months of a normal life and then everything changed, including me. Pandemic lockdowns changed me or baby number two, probably both. I went from being the hare to now hiding within my shell like the tortoise going along at a slower pace than I usually did, from an outgoing extrovert who thrived in a fast-paced environment to an antisocial and introverted shell of my former self during a lockdown and a second isolated maternity leave. It's one thing to be trapped inside your house, it's another thing to be trapped inside your head. I recently read about impostor syndrome and finally felt seen.

Have you ever looked in the mirror and not recognized the person looking back at you? Not because you changed physically but because you haven't looked in the mirror or really looked at yourself for a long time? I didn't recognize that person staring back at me—inside and out. Part of it was aging, extra baby weight, and a new hair color, but mainly it was because I hadn't taken a moment to see myself, to see beyond the surface and look into my heart. I hadn't taken a moment to check in and address my needs. I felt like an impostor in my own skin, and I doubted my skills, my knowledge, and my experience, both as a mom and in my career. I felt guilty for having two beautiful kids, a loving husband, and lots of support, while still feeling like something was missing in my life. When you no longer have a career that defines you—something that has been woven into your self-identity for most of your life—you feel lost, like there's a black hole within that continues to swallow you whole no matter how hard you try to escape it. You look in every direction, hoping to find what is missing. You pivot so much that you feel like you're spinning.

My entire maternity leave felt like a never-ending process of losing and rediscovering myself while I was trapped in my home. My internal scars felt visible, like stretch marks or curling iron burns that everyone could see. My instinct was to hide, and I did. I was holding onto negative feelings like old clothes that don't fit, staring at the drawer they were stored in, afraid to open it, and hesitant to do the unpacking required to ultimately let them go. I needed to purge, to unpack all these feelings and send this extra baggage away. I needed to "Marie Kondo" the heck out of my life. If something no longer brought me joy or pleasure, then I needed to remove it. It was time for an internal paradigm shift. It was time to change my habits, rewire my subconscious mind, and lean into my intuition. As I began to work on myself and slowly unpacked these feelings, what surfaced were feelings of inadequacy, resentment, loss, and guilt. As I doubted my past accomplishments and experience, I'd often compare myself to others who were climbing higher and faster than I was on that imaginary corporate ladder. Many were men or people who didn't have children, but we shared other commonalities, skills, and experiences. It was yet another stark reminder to me that women often deal with things twice: externally within the sociocultural constructs of society and how we "should" be, and internally when that inner mean girl keeps going, keeps amplifying the voices of others over our own inner voice. And that is the hard part—learning to quiet that negative chatter within us. And the funny thing is, that in my circle of friends, I am the one who empowers, inspires, and ignites people into their purpose, their next step. I helped them quiet their inner mean girl. Now it was time to pour this same love and support back into myself.

I forced myself to slow down, to be more thoughtful, more methodical, more vulnerable, and to take a pause. To stop and smell the roses, which I can now do in my own backyard (if I can get there before my kids pick them all). It's within these pauses that I found clarity. It's almost like everything was in slow motion and all the ideas and worries in my head moved to either side as a clear path presented itself. Now that I was making time for myself, I leaned in to be the person that I wanted to become and asked myself, How would I show up, like really show up, if perfection wasn't the end goal? I started to act like that person and showed up for myself. There were so many times where I wanted to stop and actually "Marie Kondo" my home instead, but this time I needed to put myself first. To do this for myself, for my marriage, for my family, and eventually, for my career. I finally let go of needing my house to be perfect, which reduced my anxiety, and I stopped making excuses. Who was going to see my messy house in lockdown anyway? The freedom that came from releasing this heavy expectation I had carried for years allowed me to finally experience what my husband sees when he enters a messy room—no mess at all. The kids' toys on the floor and crayon on the wall was evidence of play, and they needed this, especially now. It was my reminder to look at the mess as play, to savor the lockdown as an intentional pause, and to really create the life I desired: freedom from the hustle, doing something I loved, being there for myself and my family.

As women, we are often expected to be kind and tough (not too tough though!), sensitive and stoic (again, not too much!), a good leader and a good follower (but really, if you could be a better follower that would be perfect, thanks!), a mother, a wife, a lover, a provider, calm like a duck (because how else will you present yourself as the "good girl?"), but paddling hard underneath, with the added pressure to be perfect and have the perfect home. It is sickening. It is maddening. It is no wonder that there are so many women who experience postpartum anxiety and depression (and these present differently in each of us and don't look the same, nor is there one way to treat everyone). We wear so many hats every single day, and each hat has its own set of pressures, doubts, and fear. However, over the last decade or two, and especially the last five years, women have begun sharing boldly and more openly (#timesup #metoo #motherhoodrising), which is why it's finally starting to become normalized.

There's liberation in being raw, real, and unapologetic, and in removing those filters. What's important is that we recognize these feelings and lean in to do the work to overcome them. As women and working moms, we should be asking for equality, pay transparency, and more opportunity for career advancement, yet at the same time we are too afraid of losing our jobs and missing any promised promotions. And many of us suffer impostor syndrome and don't recognize the brilliant and powerful skills, talents, and leadership we bring to the table. We fail to tap ourselves into opportunities or even claim them. And most of all, we equate our self-worth and confidence with a masculine standard. We have been trying to be women in a world created for and still predominantly run by men. Add on the stress and anxiety of growing a human inside you while you are a working professional or even an entrepreneur, and it's a ticking time bomb. *How much time do we take on maternity leave? Do I even need mat leave? Could I just become available to work from home? This way my position at work won't be outsourced or phased out. This way I won't be phased out of a dream I worked so hard to build and achieve.*

It makes you think, doesn't it?

Yes, this is the bittersweet reality of the world we navigate. No wonder women are afraid to share their personal successes or news in the workplace. This magical time is one of fear and self-doubt as soon as you walk through those office doors. We quietly work away and hope we don't lose that promotion or opportunity because we're growing our family. We never once think to ask for it or consider that we're worth more.

When fear and self-doubt set in, I often pull strength from all the amazing and strong women in my life—especially my grandmother and my mother. My grandmother lived twenty years longer than expected due to sheer grit and a positive mindset, in my opinion. She had one of the worst cases of rheumatoid arthritis in the country and lived in constant and terrible pain. She was unable to swallow most food (Ensure was the diet du jour every day!), had crushed up meds in homemade jam, and drank the odd Kahlua at a family wedding. She raised eleven children. She was calm, resilient, and proud. It was only at night when no one was around that you would hear suffering and pain. She led with an invisible fear, a passion for life, and a strength that seemed to have no limits. My mom is much like her. After helping to raise her youngest siblings, she had a traumatic birthing experience with me, an unimaginable recovery that lasted for decades, and she pushed forward to give me a brother and to give us the life she never had, all while suffering in silence. I am always and forever grateful for my mom and all that she did, in the ways that she knew, with what she had. That's it right there—most women, including my mom, hadn't seen anything different modeled to them. "Self-care, self-love, does it bring you joy?" were not commonly accepted or embraced ideals in their generation. The self-martyrdom is what was expected of us as women, as mothers back then, and even today (no matter where you are located geographically). But us—you and me? We can change this cycle of self-martyrdom. While there is an innate beauty in doing everything you possibly can to give your children the life you never had, I'm of the thought that it should never be at the expense of your desires, your whispers, your mental and emotional health, your soul's joy. I'm of the mindset that while there will be harsh and challenging seasons in our life, and they aren't seasons that are meant to be weathered in silence alone. They are meant to be felt, heard, and explored with the ones who can hold space for you and with you.

Being an avid observer and having my own firsthand experience through my journey, I can proudly say that I don't regret any of my decisions and choices. Even the poor decisions. Especially them! If it weren't for my mistakes, my winding path and journey, I wouldn't be where I am today. I wouldn't be the woman, wife, mother I am right now. I gave everyone all of myself, so much so that I lost myself along the way. There were lessons I was destined to learn, a path I was meant to walk, and this is the person I was destined to become. The result is a more purpose-driven, people-focused, confident me. Now I prioritize my time, values, and integrity over superficialities. Now I lean into my truth, my intuition, my inner knowing, and I allow these whispers to lead me in my life, my motherhood, and my professional journey. Now I am eager to surround myself with people who have an abundance mindset, who support each other, who lead and grow with that same purpose and integrity. Daily I strive to be the best version of myself and to leave a legacy for my kids that I'm proud of while enjoying this wild ride. I want my children to know that their mother lived her joy, became one with her desires, and advocated for her needs and wants while still giving them everything she had to offer. I'm proud of what I've overcome and share my journey in the hope of helping one person who may be struggling too. You've got this; you just need to lean in, listen, and trust your intuition.

Chapter 9

FINDING SELF IN NEW BEGINNINGS

JESSICA JOHNSTONE

You get to choose the whispers you lean into; you get to choose your alignment and your evolution.

@ourlifeamongthecedars

Jessica Johnstone

Jessica Johnstone is a passionate mom to three beautifully intuitive souls, a homemaker, an educator, a holistic health advocate, an intentional mama, an organizer of "all things," a dreamer, and a nature lover. She graduated with a Bachelor of Science in Human Nutrition from the University of Guelph and went on to study all things holistic health. She is the founder of Haystone Wellness, where she supports families to embody natural wellness. Although essential oils are her main modality of choice, you won't get through a session without learning other ways to improve your physical and emotional well-being. Taking the path of an entrepreneur was not Jessica's original plan after graduation, yet motherhood quickly brought to light the importance of family, living life on her terms, and not wanting to climb the corporate ladder. Having struggled with mental illness as a mother, Jessica is dedicated to helping other moms take back their emotional well-being in all stages of motherhood. As life ebbs and flows through different seasons, she is grateful to be able to step into roles that she is being called to. At this present moment, the largest and most beautiful hat she wears is being a teacher to her two oldest daughters and a snuggle partner to the youngest. Jessica is grateful every day for the transformations and lessons that have come with wearing the many hats she never could have dreamed of wearing—homeschooling mom, wood chopper, food preserver, chicken farmer, wife, author, entrepreneur, and more. She is always ready for the next costume change.

IG: @OURLIFEAMONGTHECEDARS

To my three shining stars, Ainslie, McKenna, and Savanna, you teach me to be a stronger, more mindful and resilient mama every day. Thank you for choosing me to guide you through childhood; I am honored, humbled, and grateful to spend my days watching you explore your world. To my forever-adapting husband, Nick. Thank you for always jumping and saying YES to whatever I dream up. I cherish the life we have created and am grateful we were able to grow together. Thank you in advance for saying yes to whatever is on the horizon; we got this!

Practice listening to your intuition, your inner voice; ask questions; be curious; see what you see; hear what you hear; and then act upon what you know to be true. These intuitive powers were given to your soul at birth.

—Clarissa Pinkola Estés, Women Who Run With the Wolves

I never thought I would be affected by postpartum mental health. In fact, when our first daughter was born, I had a hard time empathizing with women who were going through that journey. *That would never happen to me. I'm rock solid.* Or so I thought. I felt like I stepped into motherhood with ease and joy. I was confident and comfortable and had minimal concerns about welcoming another little babe into our lives. It couldn't have gone more differently, and so this story really begins around the time our second daughter was born. A horribly traumatic birth left me feeling depleted, grieving the birth I thought I would have, feeling violated and disappointed in myself, and questioning everything. The initial phase of toddler and newborn life wasn't too challenging, but once our baby became colicky, things slowly went downhill for the next three years. My mental health slowly started to crumble. Over the next three years, we made quite a few family changes, started two businesses, plus my husband and I both left the corporate world and moved back to my hometown. Each of these changes were getting us one step closer to living a life in alignment, we just didn't know it yet. There were gentle nudges starting in November 2017 that were beginning to show us that change was on the horizon, but our ears and hearts weren't really listening at that point.

When we moved back to my hometown, life drastically shifted. I knew I didn't feel like myself or the version that I wanted to be but was unable to pinpoint the reasons. I remember not being able to sit with my daughters and be present with them, as it felt like a million ants were crawling all over my body, and my mind was racing with a million thoughts a second. I will never forget how it felt to appear so happy on the outside but be screaming on the inside. To truly believe that this was my new normal, the way I would live out this life. The compounding effect of multiple large life changes year after year continued to get the better of my body and soul. Instead of finding peace and healing, I felt as though I was digging deeper and deeper into a pit of grief. I had just reached a really high rank in the company I work with, we had found the perfect school for our daughters, and my husband's new business was starting to really thrive. Things were beginning to come together, or so it seemed from the outside. Inside I knew the constant need for perfection was taking a toll on those I cared most about. *What really were the most important aspects of life? Was it the beautiful home, vehicles, and keeping up with other societal norms, or were we missing something?*

Life felt hard: the crying toddler on the commute to school, keeping up with our social life, running my wellness company, being a wife, friend, and daughter—it all felt overwhelming. I knew we needed a change, but I had no idea how this change would heal my soul and change my life. I always wanted to own a big house with all the beautiful things inside. We were living in a lovely neighborhood in a home with lots of space and lots of great things going on. So naturally, when I told my husband that I wanted to trade it all in for a little cabin in the woods, he was taken aback. He needed some time to process the idea and create his own vision for the future. We had found the "perfect property." It ticked all the boxes for what I was looking for, except for one pretty big box: it didn't have a livable house. Purchasing land in September that did not have a home made little to no sense. We decided to sit on the idea and see what was available come spring. Although at the moment I knew it wasn't the right time, the pull for a change was stronger than ever. I had huge faith that the spring would bring some sort of change for us. Most days after dropping our oldest daughter off at school, I would take the long way home to drive past the property we wanted to purchase. I was able to peek in the lane and imagine what life would look like living there. I could feel it and really see our daughters growing up, running through the forest and laughing. I could hear the sound of their laughter in my ears and see the leaves blowing in the trees. I could imagine hot summer days swimming in the pond and tapping the maple trees in the spring. It was going to happen, it just had to; the *how* was the only question. I could imagine our life, feel the breeze in my hair and my feet in the dirt. A sense of calm washed over me as soon as I turned onto our road. I could feel it in my bones that life was about to change, and we were about to take a huge leap of faith.

January 2019 rolled around and with the property still on the market, I knew it was time to make it happen. Although not everyone around me, including family members, were on the same page, there was no turning back now that the vision was crafted. There wasn't another way; this was the path and journey we were meant to take.

Fast-forward to April 30, 2019, when we spent our first night sleeping in our trailer, which would be home for the next six months. There were so many things that presented as a challenge that could have made us step away, but the vision for our family was so strong that we kept moving forward through it all. The little cabin that would soon become our home wasn't much bigger than my office in our old home. We were in for a big change!

Being in the thick of emotional turmoil, I had a strong desire to hold our daughters close. Living with them and my husband in our trailer began to calm the emotional turmoil that I was dealing with every day. Moving into a thirty-two-foot trailer for six months may not be everyone's "cup of tea," but for me, it was the most at-ease I have ever felt. Let's be honest: being able to clean in a matter of minutes was a huge bonus I wasn't complaining about. Life felt like it had gotten so complicated and the things that mattered the most were suffering. Being able to spend those summer and fall months together in such a small space brought up a lot of things that needed attention and allowed the opportunity for healing and growth. There was an adjustment period, of course, as it's not every day you downsize by 90 percent. That summer was so full of laughter, smiles, pure joy, and was a huge learning curve.

Tiny living isn't for everyone, and realistically, it wasn't for me even three years ago. But life changes, we adapt, and when we surrender to what is laid out in front of us, the magic happens. What once seemed illogical is suddenly your saving grace. Tiny living also has its challenges, especially if you refurbish an old cabin and call it home. We have been faced with weeks without hot water, frozen pipes, endless construction, and shifting things around to fit, among other small inconveniences, but for some crazy reason, it still feels so good.

Emotional healing wasn't the expectation when we moved, but it was the medicine and healing we as a family needed. It was what I needed. Getting out in nature, feeling the breeze on my face and the ground beneath my feet was what I needed to shift into soul alignment. I would walk down to our pond and just sit in gratitude for all the shifts that were beginning to occur. There was magic in this place. Our land holds such an important piece of my heart, not because it is the most magical place on earth but because it was the first step of a new beginning and finding peace and ease. This land symbolized change, growth, and being rooted in aligned purpose.

The last two years have helped me become incredibly resilient and independent in ways I never thought imaginable. I grew up on a farm and quite frankly, I couldn't wait to get off it. Fast-forward to current life and one of my favorite parts of my day is doing our chicken chores. I love how the girls and I work together to care for our birds and how they get to learn so much from being a part of their lives. It has been such a learning curve for me to tend to animals in a slow-paced, child-focused environment. I find myself getting caught up in dreamland planning what animal to welcome to our lives next; even writing this down on paper seems so absurd. Me, a farmer?! The mere thought of it makes me giggle. It's ironic that our lives have never been more hectic, with three small children, animals to care for, water and heat issues, and always a million things needing to be tended to, but I have never felt so happy or nourished. Our girls often giggle at me as I walk around thanking the land for what we have, for the trees, for the water, and for the animals. I was not this person before we moved, and although I still have a long way to go, the process is magical.

Eight years into this journey of motherhood, I am amazed at how quickly and how deeply life can morph and transform once you learn to listen to that "gut instinct," a.k.a. your intuition. It's almost like the life I was meant to lead was waiting for me all along. And the beautiful souls that are our children have helped guide me in a direction that created this life. Motherhood became my biggest catalyst and my most constant whisper that led me to alignment. Growing up and even into early adulthood, I imagined living in a beautiful, large home, in an area with lots of families, places to see, restaurants to frequent, and shops to browse. Never in my wildest dreams did I imagine living in the middle of a cedar forest in a home the size of a large shoe box (okay, it's a tiny bit larger than that) with a flock of chickens and a massive dog.

Sometimes we get so caught up in the details of our day-to-day lives that we lose sight of what's truly important. We are unable to identify our challenges and areas of life that need some TLC. We continue to live on autopilot, ignoring and numbing out our experiences and emotions. I can now see that I was miserable, unhappy, and definitely not thriving. In the moment, I knew I felt anxious, but I just assumed that *this was what a mom of two little children went through*. I thought that feeling this way was "normal" and a rite of motherhood. I was unable to be present in the moment and often felt like everything was so hard. My mind was always racing, and I would do anything to escape my reality—emotional and disordered eating and locking myself away in my office to "work" (a.k.a. scrolling social media late into the night), trying to find some semblance of normalcy.

Most of my friends and family didn't know what was going on, as I became very good at putting on a brave face. The mask stayed on with a smile plastered on my face. My business thrived and from the outside, it likely looked like I was holding everything together. The desire for perfection continued to push me daily to make sure the outside world continued to think all was well behind closed doors. Until the day came when I was forced to take a look in the mirror and find at least an entry point in what would become a long-game healing journey. When we first moved, we lived in the trailer without any internet, and it felt terrifying. Yet this change couldn't have come at a better time. Spring nights were spent reconnecting with my husband, and most of all, with myself. I explored what brought me joy outside of "mom" and "business owner." I started some handwork projects, played board games, went on walks, and read a few good books.

The move really was the catalyst to opening a world of change, growth, and healing. It was the starting point of acknowledging something wasn't right. Refueling myself with lots of nourishing food, supplements, essential oils, nature, movement, and having some much-needed peace and quiet all contributed to the change. Making these adjustments are what led to the arrival of our third daughter, as pre-move I was not emotionally equipped for our family to grow. Following the path that is outside your norm really shakes things up but in the long run, it can bring about the most beautiful changes. Now I am a homeschooling mom of three and an entrepreneur who will not let my mental health struggles define me; they are a part of the journey but not the main plot. I can't say I am free from anxiety, as it does creep in from time to time. The difference now is that I feel like I have created a life that helps support my mental health and well-being and have the tools needed to help me move through it. My anxiety is a reminder to make sure I am living authentically, speaking up for what I need, and ensuring that I am not getting caught up in all the areas of life that suck the energy out of me instead of fueling the soul with passion and purpose. I now stop and listen to my emotions instead of pushing them away. I ground myself and bring my body and mind back into alignment.

Living my most aligned and authentic life right now means being out in nature, spending the days with our daughters, having messy hair and stained clothes, feeding chickens, and most likely having a face mask that is someone's lunch on my face. It means not being worried about what others think or feeling the pressure to conform to social norms. For many years it felt like we were so far out of alignment with what my soul was yearning for. We'd become obsessed with how our life "looked" and what we looked like from the outside world instead of focusing on how we "felt." Holding myself, my family, and my home to such high standards that my anxiety was all-encompassing, and for what? What was the bigger picture? What makes a family and a home whole, thriving and living a purposeful life full of vitality? Was keeping up with societal norms something that would bring us a sense of peace and fulfillment, or was it actually what was throwing us all off? It felt as though there was no room for imperfection, failure, or grace. Letting our children be kids who enjoy the simple aspect of childhood is of utmost importance in our lives.

It's been two and a half years since we began calling this place our home, and so much has changed both for us and the world around us. I have felt so held and heard by this land, so connected and supported throughout our time here. Bringing our third daughter home, renovating our cabin, raising animals, my husband going back to a corporate job, becoming a homeschooling family, and so much more. We have been thrown so many curve balls since landing here, and each time we overcome them and move forward. Life can be utter chaos, but when I look out the window down to my beloved pond, the willow and cattails blowing in the wind, all feels right. It gives me a sense of peace being held here and knowing at any moment I can get outside and listen to the vast nothingness. Waking up to no water, a frozen sink, or no heat when you are pregnant can be just about enough to throw in the towel, but all those things seem to melt away when the rest of life flows with ease. The intense feeling of not belonging, racing thoughts, and needing to be someone I am not is gone. We can live in the present moment, finding what is important to us and what will keep our family thriving and our emotional and energetic health well. The struggles and challenges were a part of the path we needed to take to find the life that was waiting for us, the life that we continue to work toward every day.

I cannot say for certain how long cabin life will continue. In fact, most days it would be easier to move back to a larger home with all the modern-day amenities. Kidding! I wouldn't trade this life for anything! A good friend has told me for years that life can be hard, but *you get to choose your hard.* Day in and day out, I will continue to choose chopping wood, dealing with freezing water, and having less personal space than desired to live a life that fills me up in so many other ways—a life that continues to give me gentle nudges that bring me closer and closer to my heart's true desires: time spent with family. What I know is that we will continue to listen to the whispers, the sometimes not-so-gentle nudges that it is time for a change, and we will honor those pulls. I now know that it is safe for us to evolve, change, and shift our path. It is something we can grow through. And who we become in the process is every bit worth it. Choosing this hard doesn't feel so hard after all. You get to choose the whispers you lean into; you get to choose your alignment and your evolution. So, get curious, get a little adventurous, and lean into the wild whispers of your heart. They aren't wild, rather they are leading you home to yourself.

SECTION 3

KELLIE BALES
JULIE KADEN
ASHLEY LOUGHEED

The resilience of the human spirit is something we don't honor enough. From the moment you come into this world, your life is a series of events and experiences. Some are more impactful than others, but they all make you who you are, in this moment. They all make up different parts of your body, mind, and spirit. Relationships are complex. They are complicated, beautiful, uplifting, depleting, and every emotion in between. Our connection to others can carry us forward or weigh us down, and it is up to us to decide how we move forward in relationships as well as outside of them. We crave connection with others: family, friends, colleagues, and lovers.

Our biggest lessons can come with huge transitions in our relationships, and those lessons allow us to navigate the path forward. Some relationships will fall short of the expectations we have and the comfort and foundation we desire from them. Some will fulfill us in ways we didn't even know we could experience. Others will teach us that grief is the price we pay for deep, loving connection.

Sometimes we will wonder how we can move on without these people in our lives. We will question whether we should be allowed to feel joy, love, a future, and whether we can let go of guilt and sadness. But all these relationships, all these endings are still with you in these moments. You aren't letting go of them, you are honoring all the lessons that brought you to this place. The power of surrender to your path— that life will catch you even when you don't know what to do yourself.

Every person who touches our life creates a ripple. Those ripples move us to expand and grow, even if there are touches of sadness or deep grief. The people in our lives create an impact, and whether negative or positive, that impact pushes us forward to who we are becoming.

Make powerful waves, big, bold moves, and listen to the whispers of your wild soul.

Chapter 10

LOVE, LOSS & LETTING GO

KELLIE BALES

Grief and loss of a life we once attached ourselves to is the ultimate portal to our greatest selves, our most compassionate selves.

@outbackgypsygems

Kellie Bales

A writer and novice wanderer, Kellie Bales spends her days consciously feeling all the feels surrounded by nature, adventure, and
creativity. She finds ancient gems in the Outback of Australia and
sends them around the world. Through her gems, writing, and
online community, she creates a space to share what grief and
vulnerability can reveal. Using her own journey with grief, Kellie
hopes to inspire others to use nature and creativity as a powerful
tool to healing and growth. Her goal is to encourage others to be
alive while they are still alive. Kellie currently resides in Western
Australia with her partner, Saxon, and their foster dog, Buddy.

IG: @OUTBACKGYPSYGEMS

To Peter—my foundation, my rock, my home. You lived your life fearlessly and fully with an understated charm and grace that was only amplified amid your terminal diagnosis. You will forever be a part of my heart and soul. I am because you were.

To my family—never have I seen a more supportive and solid network. No matter where I am in the world, you're always with me.

To Saxon—my lifeline, you made my world vibrant and colorful again. Thank you for showing me the stars and the infinite possibilities this life holds.

*We must be willing to get rid of the life we've
planned, so as to have the life that is waiting for us.*
—Joseph Campbell

I glance at my phone; it's 2:00 a.m. *My insomnia is back, again.* Ten seconds of murky consciousness clears and the reality sinks in: **The life I use to attach myself to is gone; my husband of ten years isn't breathing softly next to me.** The familiar memories flood in, and the grief is crippling at times. It takes me a few moments to orient myself. I'm not in my hometown of Newmarket, Ontario, or even in Canada for that matter, but completely on the opposite side of the globe. I'm in a tent, in the middle of the West Australian Outback, the distinct smell of wattle and eucalyptus mingling with the cool desert air. I can see all the stars and galaxies from the tent's screen window—an Outback night sky is truly something you must see to believe. The entire Universe is right there in front of you, so close you can almost touch it. I focus on one star in particular, as it seems brightest. As I watch it flicker, I wonder if it is a dying star or maybe one that died millions of light years ago. Gazing up at the stars feels like traveling back in time. I naturally reflect upon my own life and how there is light after dark, there is love after loss. I hold the warm hand lying next to me and drift back to sleep.

The weight of the grief I've experienced in my life hits me at the most random times, but mostly this weight comes crashing down on me in the middle of the night or the early morning hours when life is still and all my distractions are fast asleep. It's Mother's Day in the middle of a world pandemic. These milestone days are triggering for me and so many who have experienced grief, trauma, and loss. They are blatant reminders of what could have been, those hopes and dreams of well-thought-out and envisioned futures all destroyed—whether it's infertility, loss of a spouse, or a virus that shuts down the entire planet. Unknowingly, something was simmering under the surface, forming, growing, and spreading itself silently only to completely blindside and shatter the life you once lived, the life you had mapped out in your heart and soul. It wasn't supposed to be like this. This isn't how I envisioned my life to be. Inevitably, grief, trauma, and loss are a double-edged sword with their distinct ability to destroy and shatter dreams while also transforming us and the world around us. Everything is different. I am different, but I am here.

Life is a perpetual journey of attachment and letting go, of love and loss. My story starts with loss, as so many of them do. Loss of a life I was certain I would have, loss of the all too familiar dream of becoming a mother after years of failed fertility treatments, and loss of a spouse, my best friend and partner since I was sixteen years old. Loss creates holes or rather space, and it is here, within this space, where we have a hidden opportunity to fill the vacancy however we choose.

It is in these spaces that my ***whispers*** came.

I met my husband in high school when we were both sixteen. I know young love can come on fast and hard and is mostly irrational and immature, but I knew early on I would marry Peter. I just knew. We married in our hometown, surrounded by all our family and friends. Peter was a police officer, and I was a dental hygienist who taught yoga part time. You could totally say we were as rooted and local as they come. Life seemed to be effortless; we both had great jobs and amazing families and friends, we had recently just purchased a large, new, beautiful three-bedroom home, and we were excited to fill at least one of the rooms with a nursery, but then a roadblock occurred. For anyone reading this, if you or someone you know has struggled or are struggling with infertility, you know how absolutely life altering and isolating fertility treatments can be, not to mention exhausting and expensive. Years of failed in vitro fertilization (IVF) treatments took us to a new specialist, one who was sure to make it happen as he so arrogantly proclaimed in his over-the-top office surrounded by baby photos and thank you cards. He was right. It finally happened. I was pregnant. I honestly couldn't believe the words. For years, I had waited to hear them. But there was a glitch: the hCG levels stopped escalating the way they were supposed to. I remember the nurse looking at me after yet another daily blood draw, and her eyes said it all: "These numbers should be higher by now, but let's do blood work again in two days and we will see." An ultrasound confirmed it was an ectopic pregnancy. There had been so much excitement, followed by worry, apprehension, and frantic googling, then finally, devastation and heartbreak. I was told to go home and expect a miscarriage, yet two weeks passed and that didn't happen. At this point I was given an "emergency" infusion to induce a miscarriage. Sitting in a chemotherapy chair getting my infusion of methotrexate next to cancer patients was emotionally crippling. I drove home afterward and waited for the drug to work like they said it would, only it didn't. I felt like the Universe was playing a cruel joke. I remember thinking, *I can't get pregnant, and now I can't even miscarry properly. I felt completely inadequate and damaged.* Finally, a day surgery finalized this never-ending emotionally and physically scarring nightmare. I remember talking with Peter in the months afterward and us both deciding that this was it. Enough was enough. We would no longer invest more time, money, or energy into this insanity. We had tried, and tried, and tried again; the time had come to let go.

With our two dogs in tow, we sold our big home and downsized to a tiny heritage bungalow the size of a studio apartment, one block away from my mom and stepdad. People thought we were crazy. "Who downsizes in their thirties?!" we would hear. Our priorities were changing. We were going to travel the world and didn't want a hefty mortgage holding us back; we had made peace with it just being us. We planned this epic adventure to Bali, Australia, and New Zealand, solidifying our strengthened marriage with a vow renewal on Jimbaran Beach seven and a half years after we first said "I do." We wrote our own vows and renewed our love and commitment to one another as the sun set over the Indian Ocean. I remember thinking, *As long as I have my husband, I have everything.* It was magical.

Ten months later, Peter was diagnosed with stage four colon cancer metastasized to the liver, an out-of-nowhere terminal diagnosis that blindsided us—a diagnosis that was incomprehensible. He was only thirty-five.

There are no words for the unimaginable nightmare that followed. Peter never smoked, he went for yearly physicals with his doctor, he was young and presumably healthy, so how could someone who looked so well be so sick? A hard area on the right side of his abdomen triggered a doctor's visit. We had assumed it was a pulled muscle from coughing due to what we thought was a bad cold. On Sunday we were chatting with friends about our upcoming all-inclusive trip to Mexico, and on Monday we were being told that Peter had a large tumor in his colon and several surrounding his liver that were causing the hard area he could feel on his right side. There would be no trip to Mexico with friends. Peter would start chemotherapy two days after being told he had cancer; his advanced terminal disease was causing liver failure and therefore required immediate treatment to prolong his life. We could barely process what was going on. It all came on in such a torrent. I remember shaking so badly that my knees went weak and I could no longer stand. Our entire world was wiped out. Anyone who has experienced anything like this unimaginable reality knows that grieving begins the day the doctor tells you those words. You're grieving someone who is still here, still alive. You grieve the life you thought you would have, and you grieve the life you are forced to now live. I had so much denial and panic, and I was obsessed with trying to find anything and everything that could fix this or make it go away. Looking back, I never actually got to the acceptance stage. I know Peter did, but I couldn't, or wouldn't. I kept thinking, *Surely there's someone out there or something out there that can make this turn around.* A year and a half later, Peter was gone. So much of who I am was because of this man. How could I BE without him?

I was lost in an ocean of trauma and sorrow. As much as I appreciated the constant supportive visits from an army of family and friends, I felt like it held me back from diving deep into the newly dug hole in my heart. Although it was expected by everyone that Peter would lose his life to this disease, he never exhibited any signs or symptoms of that being a possibility in the months leading up to his death. I hadn't prepared; we hadn't prepared. Many big things were planned for Peter, most of which he planned himself and was looking forward to. The thirty hours that led to the end of Peter's life were so jarring and traumatic and shocking on a cellular level that my whole nervous system was destroyed. I can recall constantly shaking and dropping weight in the days following Peter's death. I felt like I had lost my right leg, something that had been with me my entire life it seemed, or most of it anyway. I look back on my journal entry for January 11, 2017:

"How can I continue doing what I did before, without Peter?! Everything is different now, and so am I. What do I want to do, where do I want to go?"

The truth is, I wanted to go anywhere and everywhere I could, anywhere that softened the pain, anywhere that made the vivid reminders of Peter and our life together fade. I was slowly drowning, and I felt stuck. Every time I would leave my little house, my next-door neighbor would pop outside and ask, "How are you doing, Kellie?" with that *I'm so sorry* tone and look. Even the local grocery stores would have someone wanting to give me a hug. I started to hide myself away, afraid to see anyone. My grief was at times scary and confronting to my loved ones. I knew this and would try to edit or adjust my behavior accordingly. When you're in the middle of a storm, you must have space to feel; it's intense and at times excruciating, but it's necessary. I had so much support that I felt suffocated. I felt like I couldn't fully get to the depths of my loss because I was being monitored so closely. I heard the whisper; I knew what I needed to do. In fact, if we quiet ourselves, we all know exactly what our next move is as long as we have the awareness to listen. My whispers told me the longer I stayed in my cocoon of my hometown, *OUR* hometown, the longer I would be stuck in this loop of being Peter's widow. I knew that my decision to leave would upset my family and friends. They lost Peter, now they were losing me. I almost let my love and concern for my family and friends stop me from doing what I needed to do, but the whispers became louder until I could no longer ignore them. This was about me now. In the end, I settled on a sleepy coastal town on the edge of Vancouver Island, a spot Peter and I had gone to and had fallen in love with and had even fantasized about buying a home and living in one day. This spot felt right. My heart told me Peter would approve because he loved it like I did. My dad drove me to the airport, and I started to cry. I knew everything would be different after this flight. My gut told me things would never be the same again. And, of course, my intuition was right: they never were.

Tofino gave me air to breathe—wild, fresh, clean, rainforest-fed coastal air. Air and space to simply feel it all. I went to the very beaches I went to with Peter, and I'd sit and stare out into the surf, watching the waves push and pull, surge and fall. My feelings would rise and spill out of me while sitting on those shores, then settle, a routine I got very used to. I would often wonder, *How could I have this much heartache and loss in my short life? Why me?* It was during these ocean therapy sessions that I came to realize, *Why not me?* For some reason, we move through this one life thinking that we are each entitled to a certain course or outline of how our life will pan out. We look forward to and expect only the good things, while preparing ourselves for the losses that are typically expected with time. Life is a constant surf of expectation versus reality, and I think the hardest thing for us to get past is that it isn't always going to be what we envisioned, it isn't always going to be smooth seas. These rogue storms come into our lives and destroy what we once knew to be true, and then with time and space, we rebuild and become stronger and clearer on who we truly are. The truth is that a devastating ending can ignite a new beginning.

For the first time in my life, I was completely alone. Here, there were no distractions or interruptions, just raw, quiet space to feel it all. It was painful, lonely, and deeply difficult, but that was kind of the point. I was fully "in it," and then right at the moment I thought I couldn't be there anymore, my whole life changed once again, randomly and without warning as it so often does. I received a phone call from my mom who let me know that my thirteen-year-old pug had died—the pug that Peter and I selected as a puppy together: our dog, our world. The news hit me hard, and it felt like a wound that had never fully healed had burst wide open. Another part of my heart, gone forever. The next day, while feeling particularly sorry for myself and at my lowest, I randomly and unexpectedly met a wild, free-spirited Australian surfer who was so full of life that he was electric, and slowly, my dark world began to get lighter. Life can change in a second, as we all know, but it's important to know that if you're sinking, your lifeline can come out of nowhere. You have to keep swimming; you have to hold on. My lifeline has opened my heart and mind to a world I didn't know existed before.

In the months following our random fateful meeting, I was surfing in the Pacific Ocean on a longboard, catching wild salmon off the rocks for dinner, and scrambling and jumping over waterfalls on mountain hikes I had only previously seen in movies. It was an epic adventure that then took me snowboarding in Whistler (another first), then living on a magical faraway island in the middle of the Indian Ocean called Christmas Island. I was snorkeling with whale sharks and swimming with pods of dolphins in the middle of the sea, even swimming past silky sharks! On weekends, we would hike into remote beaches surrounded by jungle with the clothing on our backs and a few tarps, and we'd sleep under the full moon surrounded by coconut crabs. It's an adventure that continues to this very day, which brings me back to the beginning, or is it the end? Camping in a tent in the Australian Outback.

Yes, life is full of decisions and possibilities as infinite as the stars in the sky. It's impossible to see it as such during our darkest times, but they are there waiting for us to notice. It all started with a calling for something radical, something different, a whisper that could have easily been dismissed or ignored. A painful ending led me to another beautiful beginning—a rediscovery of who I am as a woman, a human who has loved, lost, and now loves again. An ending can be a beginning; there is life after our most devastating and debilitating losses, but you must push yourself to get there. You must bravely let go of your old life in order to forge your new one. Grief and loss of a life we once attached ourselves to is the ultimate portal to our greatest selves, our most compassionate selves. I am forever altered and shaped by my experience of deep love and loss. Losing everything has brought me closer to myself. Let yourself love as deeply and as fully as you can and then let your heart be broken into a million pieces because you loved so very much. This really is what life is all about. I carry Peter with me every day in the pieces of my heart, and I always will. Every time I look up at the stars, I am reminded of him. We each have an inner knowing that only we know to be true. Can you hear yours? Can you feel it? Listen.

Chapter 11

LIFE BLOSSOMS BY THE BAY

JULIE KADEN

Doubting the
whisper may
silence it, but it
never disappears.

@j.stroke

Julie Kaden

Julie Kaden is a creative entrepreneur who utilizes the power of the pen for the greater good of her clients and the community. With a bleeding heart for climate change and mental health, and a passion for outdoor recreation, Julie's professional and personal life is driven by these pursuits. A mom of two young kids, she is motivated by the hope of a healthier future for the next generation. Julie was schooled at Centennial College in Toronto and holds a diploma in Film and Broadcasting. Her career has spanned the digital marketing sphere, from communications and content creation to data-driven strategies and brand building. She has also appeared on camera and in a hosting role for various events, programs, and branded content. *Whisper* is Julie's first, but certainly not last, experience as a published author. You can follow along on her next endeavor at www.jstroke.ca or @jstroke on Instagram. Julie lives in Collingwood, Ontario, where she can be found running along the trails, swimming in Georgian Bay, or shredding the slopes along the Niagara Escarpment with her husband, Ken, children, Maeve and Gage, and Brussels Griffon, Chewie.

To my mom, for paving the way toward boldness and bravery, without even realizing it. And to Ken, for being the ultimate hype-husband.

Vulnerability is not winning or losing; it's having the courage to show up and be seen when we have no control over the outcome. Vulnerability is not weakness; it's our greatest measure of courage.

–Brené Brown, *Rising Strong*

The whisper was inaudible for years. More likely, I stubbornly refused to listen to the whisper until it became a roaring call to action. I was so convinced that friends, a fulfilling job, happiness, or my authentic self would not be found in a town of 20,000. So foreign to me was the frequency of bumping into a familiar face while running mundane errands. You know, the kind you complete without thinking twice about your appearance? Wandering down grocery aisles with unkempt hair, mismatched clothes, or little to no makeup, only to bump into my dentist (*did I brush my teeth today?!*), a friend of my mom's (*is it Gladys or Glenda?*), or my nurse practitioner who, just last week, performed my annual pap smear (*awkward!*) became a regular occurrence. I longed for the anonymity city living provided and the cacophony of street sounds: the sirens, horns, and streetcars that lulled me to sleep. Conversely, the soundtrack of rural suburbia—crickets, frogs, wind-blown trees and leaves—was deafening during those long and lonely nights. It felt like a foreign land, with its inhabitants speaking a language I didn't understand. Gone was the comfort of being just another face in the crowd, vanishing amid the crowd and city smog. It wasn't until I stepped into this new place that I realized how much I loved my anonymity. The transition took years, during which time returning to life in the city was never off the table. The temptations of city life oscillated between the forefront and back of my mind—opportunities aplenty, friends who were only a streetcar ride away, concerts and live events I could attend without considering overnight accommodations in a hotel or on a friend's couch, restaurants serving my every culinary desire, and more. Collingwood, Ontario, on the other hand, felt worlds away and was small in every sense, far from the creature comforts and friendships I valued. I had subconsciously crafted my identity around things that were central to city living, and I resented my new home for what it lacked or what I thought was inconvenient. Making the transition harder was the fact that social media and the digital revolution were far from its cusp. Although I was an early adopter of Friendster and MySpace, these sites didn't offer the connection that social media does today. Even texting was relatively new, and I wouldn't own my first smartphone for another six years.

For as hard as the early days in Collingwood were, I never felt that I was above or better than it. I tried to assimilate, to find my place in this foreign space. Admittedly, I was intimidated by the close-knit community that existed here. Everyone seemingly knew everyone and by virtue, knew that I was the "new kid." No amount of time living here would give me license to use the term "local," which was fine by me, as I never thought I would ever identify as one. Those who grew up here, the true "locals," had a special kind of bond cemented with mutual memories of bush parties, nights out at the Mountain

View, and tales from Collingwood Collegiate Institute. As a very active community, those who were avid sportspeople seemed to find their fit naturally. Whereas I was clumsy, uncoordinated, and terrible at team sports. *What was I doing here? Where did I fit in?* Fresh out of school with a diploma in Film and Broadcasting, I was walking into a town whose broadcasting opportunities virtually started and ended at the local radio station—and they weren't hiring, try as I might. Ultimately, a volunteer co-op placement at the community cable station led to an entry-level production position on a daily lifestyle show that had me wearing many hats—production coordinator, camera operator, audio engineer, and occasionally, host. From there, I took on a new role as host and associate producer of my own community television show: a weekly thirty-minute magazine-style program that showcased the lifestyle in Simcoe County. This role took me to the far corners of the county, meeting and interviewing makers, growers, entrepreneurs, event planners, restaurateurs, and more. I later learned that Simcoe is Canada's largest (geographic) county and the mileage on my vehicle proved it. While crisscrossing the county for work, I had the honor of getting to intimately know the people who built their homes, lives, and families here. I often left shoots and interviews envying the passion people felt for this place and wondering why I hadn't felt that same spark yet. With a career in my field secured, a proposal from my boyfriend accepted, and our first property purchased, I was planting roots in Collingwood—but a pull to the city remained strong.

While revisionist history gave me license to romanticize life in the city, it was far from romantic while I was there. I reminisce fondly through rose-colored glasses over the things I loved about Toronto that Collingwood lacked, disregarding the parts that at times, made it unbearable. The reality is, my time in Toronto was certainly exciting, vibrant, and convenient, but it was also tumultuous. I bounced around various living situations, some more precarious than others, and not a single one felt like home. Rent was absurdly expensive, and my student budget left little room for anything but the essentials. The longest I stayed in one place was six months before a seemingly more suitable or affordable arrangement presented itself. From a Victorian mansion with twenty-six roommates to a condo with all the amenities and convenience of downtown living (but also a roommate with violent tendencies and a criminal record), to a shared house with roommates who proved to be more than just occasional smokers, drinkers, and partiers they presented themselves as, my living arrangements were about as stable as my OSAP-fed bank account.

During my final year at college in Toronto, a seemingly fortuitous opportunity presented itself that would not only relieve my financial woes but would potentially reignite a relationship that had long been strained. A last-ditch attempt to salvage a relationship with my absentee father found me living with him for my final school year. Unfortunately, even then it didn't feel like home. What was meant to simultaneously be a financial relief while attending college and an opportunity to get to know my dad despite his sporadic presence throughout my life resulted in more the former than anything else. Relieving the financial burden of paying rent was a gift I'm grateful for, especially considering my dad didn't support my mother financially or otherwise while she single-handedly raised me. Not once were funds provided for necessities. Instead, lavish gifts were presented in lieu of missed visits, skipped celebrations, and a string of disappointments. As a child, I thought these gifts were the best! A television for my bedroom at age fourteen?! Yes, please! Much to my mom's chagrin, this was not a *need,* and it led to arguments over appropriate television viewing time and content.

An electric keyboard gifted to me at age sixteen was another of many grand gestures. In hindsight, I think it was procured illegally, as not once did I ever express an interest in playing piano or keyboard. Had my dad actually taken the time to get to know me or make an effort to be around during my formative years, he would have known that I was desperate for a guitar, not a keyboard, in addition to his time, paternal affection, and some consistency. I found myself wondering why I thought things between us would be any different at the age of twenty when I agreed to cohabitate with him. Our living arrangements were physically fine, but the space we inhabited was rife with a lifetime of unspoken feelings, remorse, and tension. No longer could my love and affection be bought with gifts or material possessions. My anger simmered beneath the surface as his pattern of lies and disappointment continued. It didn't take much for my anger to manifest as rage, and a few heated discussions escalated to blow-ups where neither of us was heard and nothing was resolved. It felt like I was living with a stranger and my hopes of rekindling a father/daughter relationship were dashed. If anything, the existing chasm between us grew wider, despite the physical closeness of living under one roof. I chastised myself for being so naïve to think it could work out otherwise.

In spite of tension on the home front, I channeled my energy into my final year at school. I spent many hours around the clock in the edit bays and studio, burying my head in projects and tending to a job I landed at the school, renting and keeping inventory of camera gear. Weekends were often spent on the long bus ride to Collingwood to visit my boyfriend, Ken, who had accepted his first post-grad job there the year prior. Hailing from Ottawa, he was unfamiliar with the area, but it didn't take long for him to settle in. Coincidentally, my mom made the move to Collingwood when I moved to Toronto in order to be closer to the water. She took Ken under her wing and helped him get settled. Finding an apartment, introducing him to people, and sharing her favorite spots in this new small town were things she took great pleasure in.

By stark contrast, back in Toronto, my dad worked the night shift at Canada Post and slept most of the day. We were like passing ships, and on the rare occasion we did cross paths, the awkward silence was like helium rising within us, daring one of us to say something without hostility. I've never been one to keep things in and I wear my heart on my sleeve (for better or worse), but in those days, I bit my tongue so hard it left indelible marks. Prior attempts to have a calm and mature conversation with him inevitably escalated into screaming matches, and I no longer had the energy or desire to make this place my home or invite this person into it.

Despite our differences, I threw out a Hail Mary in the form of one final heart-to-heart where I implored my dad to help himself. Beyond my anger and disappointment, I could see he was suffering too, and if I dug deep enough, I could mine some compassion for this person who hurt me but was also partially responsible for my existence. My suggestions were all met with excuses: exercise, even a brisk walk, would "make his back hurt," healthier eating habits were deemed "too expensive and tasted like shit," and the mere notion of perhaps turning to religion was scoffed at: "I'm never fucking entering a church again." Meditation, prayer, reading, journaling, all of my suggestions were rebuked in favor of sitting in his La-Z-Boy, chain smoking and eating garbage. At the time, I took his rejection personally. It seemed so clear to me that if he gave even half a shit about himself, he could make some positive changes in his life. I now understand that he didn't want to be helped, and no amount of trying on my part would force him to change. He had to want it for himself. I wish I could have come to this conclusion sooner and without years of therapy, but such is life.

As the school year came to a close and with it, my living arrangements in the city, more false promises were doled out by my dad, including an insistence on buying me a video camera now that I had completed my diploma in Film and Broadcasting. It was a generous offer to be sure, but one that never came to fruition. Against my better judgment, I was shocked and saddened. Little did I realize that the day I graduated would be one of the last times I'd see my dad. I was in such a hurry to close that chapter and move on, physically and emotionally, that I left everything in my room of our shared Toronto apartment as was: posters on the walls, clothes in the closet, furniture intact (including the TV he gave me as a teenager, ironically). I wasn't in any rush to retrieve my belongings but never thought that was the last I'd see of them. It wasn't long after I moved to Collingwood that my dad and I stopped speaking. The odd email I received was cryptic and drama-filled. It came to my knowledge that he moved out of the apartment about a year after I'd left—of his own volition or not, I'm still unclear—and proceeded with his usual fall-off-the-face-of-the-earth stunt. By now I was old enough to decide whether I wanted him in my life and in what capacity, and history had shown me that he was not someone I could depend on. I still cared, but I kept my distance because I didn't know how to keep him in my life without caring deeply and getting hurt.

Meanwhile, life in Collingwood carried on and though it lacked the diversity and culture I so loved about the city, it provided things I would come to cherish that the city lacked. Whispers were heard in the abundance of fresh air and felt in the clean waters of Georgian Bay that I swam and played in and were only a short bike ride away. The town's unique charm, character, strong heritage, and preserved history delivered more lessons and whispers that were louder than before. I noticed a softness in its people who smiled even when they didn't know you, and under its surface, a heartbeat so strong that it connected the community. In retrospect, I came to recognize this as the feeling of home I had been seeking in the city for so long.

Collingwood grew on me, and I came to learn that big things can come from small towns. Over my nearly twenty years living here, the population has expanded by 25 percent, and with that, it has become more diverse, with more people who were just like me in the early 2000s: scared, lonely, and wondering where they fit in. My own family also expanded. The boyfriend who brought me here in the first place became my husband in 2007. In 2011 we welcomed our daughter into the world and in 2014, our son. Both kids were born and raised in Collingwood, making them worthy of the "local" moniker. Becoming a mom and raising a family here provided a level of support and connection I'm not sure I would have found in a big city. Motherhood can be very isolating regardless of where you live and having a community of new mothers and organizations that supported them was everything I didn't know I needed. The trails offered endless routes for walking babies in strollers, while the library, YMCA, and Early Years Center always had something planned, and every business I encountered in town was breastfeeding friendly. The best part? All of this was a short walk, bike, or drive away. Parking is mostly free or of low cost, traffic is generally nonexistent, and active transportation is abundant here. The same cannot be said for the city.

As for my dad, our relationship was virtually nonexistent after I moved to Collingwood. He didn't attend my wedding, never met my kids, and rarely kept in touch. I provided occasional email updates regarding my life and family but kept boundaries in place that would protect us. It wasn't until the early days of the pandemic that I received a random phone call from a Toronto Police officer who had been trying to find me for six months to notify me of my father's passing. As he was estranged from his family and didn't remarry, I was his next of kin. He died alone, in public housing in Toronto, and was found many days after he passed. He had no belongings of any significance, no legal will, and nobody by his side. This was difficult to come to terms with, especially during the spring of 2020—a time when everything felt uncertain. My feelings of immense guilt, sadness, and confusion were all-consuming. Ultimately, through therapy, I accepted that he died alone because of the decisions he made and the life he created. It wasn't for lack of trying that we drifted apart, and I'm still working to make peace with the fact that I did what I could when we lived together during my last year in Toronto. It was far from what I had hoped for, but I carry gratitude with me for what he was able to provide: a place to rest while I studied and lessons I'll carry with me for the rest of my life.

I'm grateful that I gave Collingwood a chance long enough to hear the whispers that gently guided and kept me here. That I didn't flee when I felt alone, left out, or displaced is a small miracle. I shudder to think what my life, living arrangements, or bank account would have become had I insisted on making a go of city living. While there are still many reasons I love to visit the city, it's just that—a place to visit—for I have found my home in this beautiful place called Collingwood.

The whispers that call us forward and nudge us toward our next move, destination, and desire don't always roar. They're in the fleeting moments, the gentle tug at heartstrings, the occasional sucker punch to the gut, and the dull heartache that lingers. I sat in that uncertainty and discomfort, waiting for the roar. Little did I realize it gave me what I needed most while leading me to where I belonged. Doubting the whisper may silence it, but it never disappears. Patience and curiosity give way to a gentle guide, every step of the way, along this wild and winding path of life.

Chapter 12

CONNECTING THE DOTS

ASHLEY LOUGHEED

The whispers of our heart connect us to each other, across lifetimes, life stages, and the many rites and passages of being a woman.

@girltimeinc_

Ashley Lougheed

Ashley Lougheed is the CEO and founder of Girl Time Inc., a social club for everyday women and women in business. Ashley's mission is to create a community—a Kula (*community* in Sanskrit)—for women, one where they can collaborate and create lifelong friendships, live a healthy and active lifestyle, and inspire each other to grow both individually and as a whole. She is a newly published author, a leader and a learner, with a diverse education including an honors degree in Sociology, a Bachelor of Education, a degree in interior design, and a certificate in event planning. Ashley believes wholeheartedly that it's time to connect and celebrate the rise of women as a collective vibration that is fueled with love and compassion, bravery and greatness, empowerment, and the readiness to thrive. She saw the needs, the wants, and the interests of women new and local to her town and has built a community to service those needs. At the end of the day, she is definitely a woman you want in your corner.

IG: @GIRLTIMEINC_

To my soul sister, Sabrina. You saw me, heard my whisper and believed in me before I did, and I will forever thank you for the nudge.

*I've learned that people will forget what you
said, people will forget what you did, but people
will never forget how you made them feel.*
—Maya Angelou

We held onto our babies as my husband, Darryl, gave me the "are you ready for this" eyes, and without a second thought, I popped a bottle of champagne, toasted to new beginnings, and called our families with the news: "We are coming home!"

Being true believers in the divine world of non-coincidental coincidences and the workings of fate, we would witness our whole world change in eight days and send us on a new direction that would connect all the dots.

May 28, 2015, our SUV was loaded with my bridesmaid dress, shoes, and a month's supply of baby and toddler stuff. The trip to Ottawa from our home in London, Ontario, would take about nine hours, accounting for all the stops along the way and with my four-month-old son, Everett, and almost four-year-old daughter, Lillian. The big road trip was for my lifelong best friend, Devon's, wedding. At the same time, Darryl was staying in a hotel a block away from us and preparing to write the biggest exam of his life. Needless to say, life was full.

Traveling to Ottawa was like traveling home to a city and a time period that we referred to as the glory years of our adulthood and had previously lived for four years. Right before we left for this road trip, Darryl took our first leap of faith and applied for an orthopedic position in our hometown of Collingwood, Ontario. We knew that this position was rare and that if he didn't apply, he would regret not seeking out the opportunity.

At that time, it wasn't common that an orthopedic resident, fresh out of residency and exams, would enter the work world without completing at least one fellowship, a fellowship that we had already planned out and would start on July 1, 2015. Still, it did not hurt to apply. We were supposed to move to Toronto for a year and then out to Banff, Alberta, for an additional year. We had the moving trucks, the Toronto apartment lined up, and all the mental preparations of moving in motion. We were also still in the slowest housing market; our home was listed with zero offers.

We returned home after a packed weekend of wedding bliss and exam fatigue and our world flipped, swirled, and got completely swept away in a new direction, a direction we didn't see coming and were not prepared for. That Monday, Darryl got the message that he had an interview, so he traveled to Collingwood for it, then our house sold, and Darryl got the job. All within the span of one week. Talk about change sweeping in.

Following the fast flow of change, one step in front of the other and in full trust that it would all work out, we had twenty days to make the change from moving to Toronto to now moving to Collingwood. When you only have a short window of opportunity, you have to make quick decisions. With no home to move into, we also quickly sought help from our families to find us a home.

My dad, being the Monopoly player and a true king of the game, jumped at the opportunity to buy and flip a house, something that he apparently has wanted to do for a while, and this gave him the nudge to do it.

Everything fell into place. Darryl's parents were our safe landing space and cushion while all the renovations took place, and in a very short period of time, we moved into our new home right before our daughter turned four in July 2015.

Moving "home" was not a part of the plan. Or so my husband and I thought. We left home when we were eighteen and, at that time, looking back was not an option. My high school years had their fair share of highs and lows and leaving it behind was more a relief than it was a longing to return, for me at least. My acceptance into university offered me an exit, one that I happily took and packed for eagerly. It was an opportunity to start fresh and a place for me to truly rediscover who I am and who I wanted to become.

We left home and were almost thirteen years away from our childhood communities. Three cities, four to five years in each city, and now we were returning home with a whole new version of ourselves plus two young children. The saying "The only constant in life is change" rang true in my ears.

The assumption made by many was that it would be an easy transition for us to move back home. We were both born and raised in the area, our families were rooted in the community, we were connected, and we had several of our childhood friendships still residing in our hometown. I knew better, though. Who I was when I left the town at eighteen and who I was returning at thirty-one were not the same, but neither was our town. Our return would be as different as we were and that was the next big adventure we would take.

Like the other cities though, we were the newbies, the transients. We had to re-ground ourselves, set up our home, figure out where to shop, meet our new neighbors, re-establish ourselves with old friends, make new friends, and find our sense of home. Being self-proclaimed veterans to this, having moved several times and knowing the "ropes" of being the new girl, I knew the drill and how to find my place within our new community.

This time, however, I relied on help from some old friends, family members, and all the memories of being a small-town girl. I still knew all the streets and the running routes, and although my memories of people's names proved to be horrible, their faces were familiar, and I could work with that.

Our first-year home was full of figuring out where we belonged and who we connected with. I knew that one strategy for finding our footing was to get involved in events, socials, and activities that always sparked my interest and tended to my needs, wants, and joy. This is where I found and made new friendships and had the opportunity to rekindle old ones.

I trusted the process and started to align myself with people who had commonalities and shared interests and who were like-minded as I was. I ran into an old high school friend, Jen, and after a half an hour of easy conversation, it felt like no time had passed. We exchanged numbers and made plans to meet for coffee and a playdate with our two little men, just months apart in age. A simple connection led to a heart-opening friendship and one that we both needed.

At the bachelorette party of my friend Laura from London, I was reintroduced to her soon-to-be sister-in-law and another high school acquaintance, Jackie. Instantly, we clicked. We understood each other's language and what I was looking for in a friendship was delivered, along with a shared love for champagne. She made having a friend easy with her no-nonsense, show-up-as-you-are, be-a-voice-and-not-an-echo style to friendship. A true breath of fresh air.

Knowing that I needed to create some quality "Ashley time," I joined a running clinic that was hosted through my husband's new office. That is where I met another Jenn, and she would soon connect me to her group of "go" kind of women. Jenn's introduction led to being invited to participate in a 10k + mud obstacle race up Blue Mountain with a team of "Wonder Mommas" (our team's name). We not only crushed that race, but we did so laughing, rapping gangster songs, and jumping over walls, all while completely covered in mud.

One by one, I started finding my people and making heartfelt connections. Being back home was proving to be the best change with the brightest new start, and I was finally seeing a glimpse of myself, one that I had long forgotten during the early years of motherhood.

Three hundred and seventy-five days after moving home and after viewing twenty-five houses in the hope that we would buy our next home, we found, purchased, packed up, and moved, again on the day our daughter, Lillian, turned five.

I was beginning to see and feel like things were aligning. Every decision I made felt effortlessly easy. A total state of flow. I was following my sense of self and trusting my heart along the way.

I found happiness in the newfound friendships that I was dedicating time and energy toward, as well as in my reconnection with family. One of the best perks of coming home was that I got to spend quality time with my three nieces and my soul sister, Sabrina. My chosen sister. Her beautiful little girls, who I held as infants and would always travel home to visit, were now young ladies—old enough to babysit my two kids, and on a weekly basis.

These weekly babysitting hours gave me the freedom to invest in my own time to regain my own identity as *Ashley* while giving me the time to pursue and make my return to education. This time round, I didn't return to the education system and my "teaching" backyard. This time, I followed my heart's passion for interior design and event planning.

I knew that these degrees and programs would be my stepping-stone to opening the door to more opportunities. I completed one degree, only to begin the other. Again following the whisper to change my professional direction and go after "more," these programs propelled me toward what I had been dreaming of my whole life and the new route I would take to get there.

With this new community of women surrounding me and participating in socials and activities with me, I soon noticed that we shared a collective need and desire for girl time—time away from our responsibilities as adults and motherhood, and in a space that we felt welcomed, seen, heard, and valued, where we were called by our first names, and most importantly, where we had fabulous fun together. We were writing our own adventure stories and a light was shining so very bright within us!

I was happy! I was making connections and developing tightly knit friendships; I was a social butterfly spreading her wings and spending quality time with other amazing women. I was fully involved in my children's worlds, my nieces' worlds, and in organizing playdates, activities, adventures, and socials for them, for the mothers, and for myself. That is when I had *the* idea. It was my eureka moment, if you will, one that would create a ripple of change that came in the form of yet another whisper.

I had the house, the know-how, and the life experience of years of either hosting or participating in socials, and I was in a position that I could host epic girls' nights. I dreamt it up, collected all the supplies, created the invitations, and referred to these parties as "Bubbles" parties, named after the ridiculous amount of champagne I bought and showered the ladies with.

During a conversation with my cousin's wife, who had recently become a consultant to an up-and-coming handbag company, she shared with me that she was nervous about being a "sales rep." I knew she needed the opportunity to strengthen her skill set and confidence and to feel safe in a room with a group of women—a task that is not always easy. That is when I added to the "Bubbles" experience where women in business were recognized, seen, heard, and experienced in every way. I provided them with a space where connections would be made and where businesses would shine by giving them the platform to showcase their merchandise to their target audience, which just so happened to be in my house.

I started hosting these amazing Bubbles events and, inadvertently, started changing the path for many other women in their businesses and in their own identities.

Each time I hosted an event, I leveled up and made it bigger or added a twist. I combined the women who needed a night out *and* the women who needed an audience to introduce their product. One of the events turned out to be a full disco light dance party in my cleared-out living room. Another event turned out to be a Zumba-meets-yoga night, which I hosted after feeling inspired by my friends, Becky, a new consultant to an athletic apparel company, and Jessica, who was reintroducing herself as a yoga instructor in our area. With the right music, the welcoming atmosphere, and the product in motion, I served up champagne and charcuterie boards to more than forty ladies that night.

After hosting Bubbles parties and other collaborative events, my relationships with these women grew into a full support, "long-house" effect. We had each other's backs, fronts, and everything in the middle, and we held each other up. We were connected.

On November 24, 2018, I combined everything into one fabulous party and a party that would mark another moment in time when my world shifted and created a new dot.

A party like this does not get planned out overnight. Fully knowing the grand vision was bigger than myself, I surrendered and leaned on my two girlfriends for help. We spent months creating, planning, shopping, and putting to life "Ladies Evening Market with Bubbles."

My house was cleared out to make space for twelve vendors to set up their mini shops. We invited an inspiring woman guest speaker, we made a runway for a local fashion house to put on a fashion show as entertainment, and we catered the night with food and champagne-inspired beverages, opening up my home for a night of celebration.

Being that it was at the end of November and so close to the holiday season, we asked every woman walking in my front door to pay it forward with a donation of a nonperishable food item, money, and/ or an unwrapped toy. It was our version of a social enterprise: do good by doing good.

Everyone was there. All my close girlfriends, new ladies to the neighborhood—I even had my best friends from Ottawa and London travel to take part. Sabrina and my niece were in attendance, along with Sabrina's two best girlfriends. My house was full of women who were laughing and chatting and who were all dressed up and ready to just "be."

Before the night took off into a full dance party and before I made my speech to the audience of women, I popped a special bottle of champagne and poured three flutes—one for Sabrina, one for Lauren, and one for myself and toasted our bright future together.

Speaking comes naturally when I am passionate about the topic. This particular speech came directly from my heart.

I said,

"To all the ladies here in this house! Each and every one of you has a reason for being here. You might have needed a girls' night, a night away from your children and/or partner. You might have been simply curious. Maybe your reason is to let go of something that weighs on you and needs a little support from friends. OR you love champagne and want to dance! Whatever the reason, tonight we support you and that need, and we thank you for coming!

Lastly, my mark on 2018 starts with a quote from Maya Angelou. She said, 'I've learned that people will forget what you said, people will forget what you did, but people will never forget how you made them feel.'

Tonight, our only wish is that all of you feel powerful, beautiful, inspired, supported, and loved from a night out with girlfriends and a couple bottles of champagne. Cheers!"

Three days later, the house was cleaned and put back together, pictures and stories were posted, and all was right in the world. Everyone's hangover was cured, all but one. Sabrina, still feeling ill and unable to recover from a migraine, went to see her doctor and called me directly with the results. Back story: Early that year, she had been cleared of cervical cancer, a battle that she fought for almost five years. This headache that would not go away was a result of cancer that had metastasized to her brain.

Time spent together, with her and her girls, was now my only priority. I stopped everything. No more parties, no events, and activities would shorten too. Quality time when time was running short.

On a spring afternoon in May 2019, Sabrina and I had made plans to spend time together. Some much-needed girl time. A day to do some window shopping, have a lunch date at a café where I'd share all the details of my upcoming business ideas, and take a trip to a local shop for a tarot card reading.

A typical day spent with a girlfriend would lead to a swift shift in my direction. If I listen deeply enough, close my eyes, and truly transport myself back to that lunch date at the Heaven Café, I can still hear her voice telling me to search within my heart and hear the whisper that she already knew existed. I can hear her laugh as she gave me a snapshot of a journey I'd go through, only to find out that this whisper would be one of my life's biggest purposes.

"Oh, Ashley," she said, while laughing. "It is so much bigger than that."

I was sitting across the table from my soul sister, who saw into my future, gave me the nudge, and made me feel like I was truly seen, the only way a true friend can, fully knowing what she was experiencing was now coming to an end and in that moment in time, was beyond my sight.

It was time to connect the dots, link the community of women, and listen to the biggest whisper of all. The whispers of our heart that connect us to each other, across lifetimes, life stages, and the many rites and passages of being a woman. The whisper that echoes through each of us, if only we take time to listen, to see it in each other, and in ourselves. The whisper that allows us to feel our way into our next big leap, our soul path, our soul mission, right alongside our soul sisters.

SECTION 4

ALLISON VILLA
KIRTI WHITE
AMY MILNE
KIRSTI STUBBS

There is looking back and then there is being very afraid to move forward. Our whispers are often there to help us know when to move forward and when to pause and reflect. Sometimes we can only see how we followed our intuition and the whisper we listened to when we take a moment and look back on our lives. Other times we are so focused on how things used to be or what we didn't do that we drown out the whispers in our present moment that we are so desperately searching for.

The women in *Whisper* have used reflection and self-awareness as their potent fuel for motivation. Bold, brave women get real with themselves about their behaviors, actions, and fears. Call it "self-development" if you must label it like a section in a bookshop, but the reality of pausing, witnessing, understanding, and choosing to go forward with more awareness and intention is something each of these women have done the work on. And they continue to do so. They use their insights to grow and evolve so that they can take inspired action—despite what someone else says or what they have always done—to create an unconventional life that makes them feel alive!

We all have a lot going on in our lives—the day-to-day jobs of keeping a home, managing a family, and having relationships, marriages, and aging parents fill our days, and on top of that, we have hobbies, passions, careers, and businesses. It is not surprising that many women struggle to create a consistent practice of meditation and/or journaling. It can be overwhelming to add more to our to-do lists. Then there is the reality that doing this work affects our emotional state and sometimes that ripples into our mental health and our capacity. We have all had a week where the moon is just right for a big release, and we have no choice but to feel all our big feelings. We cry without knowing why we are crying exactly and then require twenty hours of extra sleep or a day off with a migraine. So, it is not surprising that some women avoid this work altogether because it can feel like a lot to process. For so many reasons, making space and time to reminisce, reflect, and assess our lived experiences is not always prioritized or possible. However, when we pause long enough to really reflect—on past relationships, past jobs, our childhood, interests—we begin to notice things we didn't see in the moment.

For some, looking back is best done with a therapist or coach. A trusted guide who can both gently ask you the right questions and create a safe environment for processing. Others will get a kickstart from a juicy tarot session or Reiki. Most people find value in writing with carved out space and time, a great pen, a beautiful journal, and a series of thought-provoking questions to have a deep and insightful reflection. This journaling becomes a tool for having radical honesty, articulating emotions, recalling past experiences, and uncovering fears or limiting beliefs. It also gives us the ability to "zoom out," and with that perspective, we start to see the bigger picture, connectedness, themes, and how the full story comes together.

Curiosity is powerful. Self-reflection is powerful. Knowing the lessons we've taken away, what we are grateful for, any synchronicities, even the miracles we have witnessed in our lives—these are all powerful things. They build confidence and feed our trust by reminding us that when we felt uncertain in the past, things all worked out. That even the most shattering moments taught us something and life is filled with "didn't see *that* coming" moments. That there are no real failures, only opportunities or redirections. That we are stronger than we know. A caveat: When we agonize over the past, it can keep us stuck. If you are feeling stuck in the what ifs or the regret, then it is time to help yourself let go, forgive yourself (and anyone else—yes, even if they don't "deserve" it), or the big one—trust that where we are now is exactly where we are supposed to be. Look back, glean what you can, but don't linger.

Make powerful waves, big, bold moves, and listen to the whispers of your wild soul.

JOURNAL ACTIVITY

In the back of the book, we have included a series of questions to guide you in a beautiful journaling practice to help you reflect. There are no rules—you may sit down in an afternoon and race through it or you may work through these over six months. Be real and honest with yourself, embrace your emotions, look for the whispers, and trust yourself when unexpected things come up as you do this powerful work.

Chapter 13

FROM DISCOMFORT COMES GROWTH

ALLISON VILLA

Your desires
will feel
uncomfortable,
like shedding an
old skin for a new
one. Do it anyway.

@allison__villa

Allison Villa

Allison Villa is a psychotherapist, relationship expert, creator of The 4 Relationship Seasons™, and host of the *Couplehood* podcast. Her honest approach to parents in love has impacted couples, and families, worldwide. As a wife and mother, she understands how raising a family affects the romantic relationship and the challenges that modern parents face. With Allison's virtual therapy practice and online offerings, this "keepin' it real" mama combines her personal and professional experience to teach busy couples how to stay connected, to have clear communication, and to build an intentional life for their family. Allison has been featured on numerous podcasts, blogs, and media outlets, including *Breakfast Television* and CBC.

Her mission is to build a movement of parents-in-love, because how you love each other today will live on through your kids and in generations to come. Find out your Relationship Season by taking the free quiz at www.allisonvilla.com

IG: @ALLISON__VILLA

For my parents: Thank you for giving me the solid roots that gave me the confidence to fly my own unique path.

For Arjan: Sharing this journey with you makes life so much sweeter. Here's to many more years of adventuring together.

For Haleh and Teah: May you always listen to your own whispers and follow your truth. Keep shining your light, my loves.

If you are going down a road and don't like what's in front of you and look behind you and don't like what you see, get off the road. Create a new path!
—Maya Angelou

THE QUIET AWAKENING

It was spring, the transition of the season ever present. The mornings felt cool, and by the time it was noon, it felt as warm as summer. I was at my university library, patiently waiting in line for a computer. (This was before everyone carried their own laptops, tablets, or computers in the palm of their hands.) I was twenty years old. A high-achieving student, active in extracurriculars, and recent valedictorian of my high school class. Until that moment, I had never stepped off the well-marked trail. I was privileged to be studying at the post-secondary level, had worked hard to get there, and was immensely grateful for where I was.

But what was this growing feeling of discomfort within me? There were rows upon rows of students sitting in front of computers. It was silent except for the sound of their fingers tapping on the keys. It felt eerily robotic. Like I didn't belong.

This wasn't where I was meant to be.

I had grown up studying classical piano, singing in choirs, and competing in high-level dance competitions. My affinity for the arts was an integral part of who I was, and yet I had learned along the way that you can't make a living doing *those* things. So, instead, here I was, doing the things I "should" be doing, and lining up to join the masses.

Nope. No, thank you. Not doing it.

To say that I floated out of my body would be an understatement as I found myself stepping out of the line and walking straight into Registrar Services, tears flowing. *What is happening to me right now?* I announced that I'd be finishing the year and then taking a break from school.

I knew where I was meant to be.

Finding my way back to joy, to expressing myself through movement, and song, couldn't be suppressed any longer. I auditioned for multiple musical theater programs in my province. It didn't matter if it made sense to anyone else. It made sense to me. I had already "quit" dancing when I was in high school, and I missed it tremendously. Of course, I had done so in order to focus on my academics and school-based extracurriculars . . . all with the desire to be responsible and follow the conventional path of life that was expected of me. But even then, I had a voice always whispering, *Why not me? There are artists, dancers, and musicians who are incredibly successful and doing what they love, so why not me?* Yet, sociocultural pressures would swarm in and squash that niggling whisper.

So, I left university to do what filled my soul. There I was, finally free from the confines of traditional classrooms and at home in the creativity of dance studios, music practice rooms, and onstage bliss. My twenties were spent touring the world as a performer, working on cruise ships and, in between adventures, teaching dance and waiting on tables. I bought my first home at age twenty-seven with the savings I had earned from being a performer. By listening to my inner voice, I had learned that being an artist could indeed bring me both joy *and* success.

From discomfort, comes growth.

Go inward.

Listen.

The answers you seek lie within.

Let your whispers speak to you.

Within them lay the stepping-stones toward finding your joy and living your truth.

The whisper was powerful. And I am thankful I found within me the courage to listen to her and follow her lead.

FROM BREAKDOWN TO BREAKTHROUGH

It was the end of April.

I was slowly emerging from the blues that had plagued me since becoming a mother five years earlier. I felt like a shell of the fun, vibrant woman I used to be.

On that gray, wet, dull day, I had five consecutive kid-free hours between drop-off and pickup. This meant that I would be running around all day doing errands and would be exhausted by the time I picked up our kids, ages three and five.

The to-do list raced through my mind:

We just ran out of toilet paper . . . need to buy that!

Our eldest needs new indoor shoes for school . . .

Dinner needs to go in the Crock-Pot before noon,

and today was the last day that I could return the lightbulbs (I bought the wrong ones . . . again . . . ugh).

I was thirty-six years old. On the surface, I had the dream life: Within the past five years, I had met and married my amazing husband, had been blessed with two daughters, had bought a home (and renovated it), and simultaneously had gone back to school for my new vocation as a psychotherapist. To say that it was an eventful five years is an understatement.

I had recently earned the professional designation of "registered psychotherapist"—a process that had taken seven years in total. It was a finish line that had seemed unreachable during those years with two young children. It was SO MUCH WORK. Years of in-class studies and endless hours spent one-on-one with clients and with supervisors, not to mention staying consistent with my own personal therapy sessions. The only class that I wasn't able to attend in all those years was on the night that our first daughter was born. If I'm being honest, between navigating new motherhood and my new career, I had been spread pretty thin. But I did it. I got that professional designation. It was the final piece of the life puzzle that would solidify my success as a full-fledged adult. I thought that it would make me feel successful, complete, or at least less overwhelmed.

Why did I not feel fulfilled?

There she was again, that whisper, that growing feeling of discomfort. This time, her roots had grown deeper. Because this time I knew what it felt like to be ME—fulfilled, full of joy, vibrant energy. When you know how you desire to feel and your life no longer feels like that . . . it can be a gnawing feeling that continues to eat away at your heart.

I could already see how the day would unfold—I would pick up the kids, eventually tear them away from the school playground, prepare dinner as they found various ways to annoy each other (I love them like crazy, but let's keep it real), and my husband would walk in the door as it all came to a roaring climax. Amid the chaos, we would pass the proverbial parenting baton, then I would frantically rush out the door to work for the evening at my private practice.

I had become the mean mom and resentful wife. *How? When did this become me? There had to be more to life than this, right?* The thought of continuing this cycle left me in a dark, dark hole. I couldn't ignore the discomfort. I had to listen to this whisper and speak my truth.

That night, my husband and I began the most life-altering conversation of our lives. It was a pivotal moment when the fate of our marriage was palpable. *If he was genuinely happy with our current life, would this conversation lead to the end of our marriage?*

To my great relief, he shared that he, too, had a similar feeling of dissatisfaction. We agreed that time is the most precious resource of all. We didn't want to wait until retirement to have quality time together and to travel . . . we wanted our children to experience the world beyond our nine-to-five routine.

Why are we taught to work the hardest in our fittest and most mentally alert years, and to wait until we're sixty-five to live our best life? There must be a more balanced way to live!

The conversation left us both (re)energized, connected, and hopeful for what was to come. The more we talked, the more our values and vision came into focus, until eventually we made a decision to spend the following winter in Mexico. Yes, a four-month family sabbatical!

That winter we lived in Puerto Escondido, Mexico, in a tiny two-bedroom apartment where we cooked all our meals on a two-element hot plate. We walked barefoot to the beach every day, drank fresh coconut water, and embraced a slower-paced life. We were also challenged in more ways than we could have ever imagined, and with that came immense personal growth.

With that personal growth came the realization that we couldn't go backward . . . going back to our old life no longer felt in alignment. Because when you leave the box you once thought you had to confine yourself to, you will never desire to crawl back in. We were stepping more and more into our truth and loved this wholesome way of living. So, we conjured up a new plan: fly back home, as planned, then drive our Nissan Sentra—complete with our family of four and all our belongings—all the way to Mexico and live there for the year.

And so we did just that. The following year we drove (and tent-camped en route) from Canada, through the United States, all the way to Oaxaca State in Mexico. The girls went to an incredible school in Puerto Escondido where they were immersed in Spanish, my husband and I built a thriving online business, we met incredible people, and most importantly, we made beautiful memories adventuring as a family.

From discomfort, comes growth.

Go inward.

Listen.

The answers you seek lie within.

When your whispers ask that you pack up and leave behind the life you once knew so that you can create the life of your dreams, do it. You will be one step closer to living in alignment with your heart's desires, your truth.

WINDS OF CITY AND COUNTRY

It was late spring of 2020.

We had driven home from Mexico the previous summer and just when we were finding our flow again in Canada, the world shut down. The city that we had loved for twenty years no longer felt like home. The four of us were trapped inside the confines of our semidetached house and our postage-stamp backyard (albeit any outdoor space is a novelty in the city). The girls, now six and eight years old, had been home from school for many months. We wanted to be present for them through this challenging time, so early on we had decided that my husband would stop working and take on the role of caregiver. We had foregone our (brief) attempt at online school, and he took on homeschooling them like a champ. The dead-end back alley that had once been our kids' go-to for social time with neighborhood friends had become a political mess of rules and social distancing. It was heartbreaking. The social anxiety was palpable.

There it was again, that growing feeling of discomfort. And this time, she was roaring, shoving, fighting back. No. More. Confinement. Period.

But what could be done? Everyone was feeling discomfort. It wasn't just us. The difference was that we had the advantage of recently experiencing an incredible, life-changing family adventure. The resiliency, confidence, and growth that came from embracing that lifestyle change was still fresh.

You did it once, you'll do it again. Here, too, you will find your truth. Go!

First, my husband and I used realtor.ca as an escape, to dream about life outside of the city. We were exploring options, but the city had always been a safe landing place for us and moving away from familiarity felt scary. We weren't ready to make any big changes . . . yet.

In June, we were finally allowed to stay overnight beyond the city limits. We used the opportunity to explore rural property listings with our real estate agent and to have a visit with family whom we hadn't seen in months. The only accommodation we could find en route was a cozy yurt on a biodynamic farm. We were already experienced tent-campers, so we welcomed the opportunity to "glamp" in a yurt!

Upon our arrival, the girls disappeared to explore the farm. It was the first time in months that my husband and I had some space from them. To our delight, when the girls found their way back to the yurt, there was a renewed brightness in their eyes. Their excitement and wonder about all the facets of the farm had brought out something in them that I'd never seen before.

This is the way kids should feel. This is the way all humans should feel. Free. Full of life and vitality. Radiant.

We met our gracious hosts, and the next morning over a farm-fresh breakfast, they told us more about the area. As it turned out, there was a local school that was in alignment with our values. From there, the vision became clearer. *This is the area where we're meant to move!*

But wait . . . MOVE?! *Were we actually going to leave our urban life?!* I mean, we had moved to Mexico, but that was temporary. This felt permanent and took our discomfort to a whole new level. We were, after all, "city people." We rode our bikes everywhere, loved multiculturalism, frequented live theater and live music, and walked to farmers' markets.

Were we ready to make the move to country life?

Despite our doubts, we kept coming back to the feeling of freedom, joy, and radiance that we had all experienced at the farm. It felt scary, but we went ahead and hired a real estate agent to list our house in the city. The day the painters came to prep the house for staging and photos, our belongings were piled under sheets in the center of the room, and the reality of our decision to move became SO REAL.

Why are we choosing this chaos? This is hard and uncomfortable. Maybe we should just stay. And wait. But that whisper that we were creating a life of greater alignment kept us moving through the discomfort.

Another challenge was that we hadn't found a new house (despite making multiple offers), and the prices continued to soar. It's hard to make the leap when you don't have a clear vision of where you'll land. Things were not "falling into place" in our search for a new home, but there was that feeling again . . .

Grow through it, Allison. You will find your home. Lean in.

Our home in the city sold in July. Needless to say, it was extremely emotional. Seeing the sold sign on our front lawn was difficult. Our youngest daughter was born in the master bedroom, my father had renovated the space for us, and we had so many family memories there. There was so much grief through the process. We were shedding one identity, one way of life, to embrace a way of being that felt truer, more us, and yet was also new and unknown.

Since we still hadn't found the right property to purchase, we settled on a lovely rental as a transition place. This meant that the girls could begin at their new school in September, and it would be easier for us to see newly listed properties in a timely manner.

Finally, at the end of September, the cards aligned (well, almost!)—we found a 600-square-foot cabin on the Saugeen River on four acres of land. It was perfect, except for the 600-square-foot part. Working from home meant that we would need a little bit more space. Thankfully, it was in our budget to do an addition.

As I write this chapter, our addition is nearly complete (after fourteen months of designing and building), and our family is on schedule to move to our River House in the new year. Since moving to this area, we have met an incredible community of like-minded families, we have found a wonderful (slower) rhythm as a family, and we are enjoying the access to nature during all four seasons.

I'm so glad that we made the leap, even though it was the most uncomfortable of them all.

The way I see it, following our inner compass won't always look or feel comfortable. It's a combination of highs, lows, and everything in between. It's learning to process grief for the ending of a chapter that has been filled with purpose and learning, while simultaneously feeling grateful for the next new chapter that is in the process of being written.

We are born into this one life with a blank canvas. As we grow up, our canvas has been painted with a variety of textures and colors, courtesy of sociocultural norms and expectations combined with our own diverse blends of family history, expectations, desires, dreams, and more. We live on this permanent, shiny, goal-post syndrome and keep moving our true desires to the back burner. The proverbial rat race, golden handcuffs, will continue to dazzle us unless we consciously choose to check out of it. Choose *us* for a change. Our hopes, dreams, and desires.

How do you want to feel? What are the internal rules that you have written for yourself? How can you break those shackles and truly listen to your own desires?

Yes, we each have our own versions of the invisible finish line. The "thing" that will make us happy. However, life is not a series of if/then/when trade-offs. The Universe doesn't work that way; it responds to wholehearted desires and action in alignment with those desires.

Your desires will feel avant-garde, out of the norm, and unattainable at times. Lean in anyway. Grow through it anyway.

Your desires will feel uncomfortable, like shedding an old skin for a new one. Do it anyway.

Your desires will often require you to forge your own path; lean in anyway.

They will require you to drown out the noise around you so that you can listen to the whispers of your heart. If it feels a bit scary, then you're on the right track. You are brave and bold, and you were born to live in alignment with *your* truth, no one else's.

From discomfort, comes growth.

Go inward.

Listen.

The answers you seek lie within.

Chapter 14

SIMPLE HAPPY LIFE: LIVING ABUNDANTLY WITH LESS

KIRTI WHITE

Lean in, pay
attention to your
breath, your body,
your heartbeat,
and your energy—
they will show you
exactly what you
need.

@kirtiwhite

Kirti White

Kirti White grew up on Salt Spring Island in the beautiful Gulf Islands of British Columbia, Canada. Her childhood was filled with adventure in the 100-acre woods beside her childhood home, feasting on the abundance of fruit, vegetables, and nuts from her parents' farm, regular exploration of the provincial parks throughout British Columbia with her parents, and world travel. In school, she studied Outdoor Recreation Management and to that she added becoming a yoga teacher and a life coach. She recently enrolled in school to become a Counseling Psychologist. She has passion for yoga, learning, outdoor recreation, travel, personal development, minimalism, essentialism, slow living, and helping people find happiness in their lives. She lives with her two children and their pet budgie in Vancouver, British Columbia.

IG: @KIRTIWHITE

For my two amazing children, Takaya and Logan.
You are my inspiration and my motivation. You bring
a smile to my face every day. Your light has helped
me face any obstacle with determination and helps
me focus on the good around me. In this life, you will
face challenges; when you do, look for the positive
and keep your attention there. There is a reason
for everything. Sometimes it is hard to see or to
understand what that reason is until you are on the
other side. Trust in your intuition and design a life that
brings you happiness.

Do not worry that your life is turning upside down. How do you know that the side you are used to is better than the one to come?

—Rumi

FAMILY OF DOERS

I was born into a family of doers. My parents are some of the hardest working people I know. My dad's nickname is Doozer, a nod to Jim Henson's ever-busy *Fraggle Rock* characters, though both my parents could equally share this name. My parents worked and played hard. They alternated between work weekends on their farm and relaxing weekends when we rose early and spent the day filled with activity. Vacations were wilderness-destination-driven and activity-filled. It was fun! Our family lived a full life. However, taking time to pause and relax was not practiced.

When I was twelve, this fast-paced lifestyle changed when my parents took six months off work to travel and explore five different countries in Southeast Asia. They wanted to give me a childhood of abundance that they had never had and to experience the beauty of the world through activities and immersion in other cultures. A rough travel plan was created, and we left on our adventure. Our first destination was a remote island in Malaysia. As soon as we got there, my dad crashed from exhaustion. For two weeks my dad spent most of his time sleeping, his body fatigued from years of nonstop activity. I now believe he had adrenal fatigue, and as soon as he gave himself a moment to relax, his body went into repair mode, forcing him to sleep and slow down. This set the pace for the rest of our trip. When we returned home from our travels, taking time out to slow down was honored. However, little by little, our lives became busier, and we all returned to living rich, full lives.

In high school, I learned that working hard was rewarding. I was driven. As a young adult I worked hard, played hard, and studied hard. One summer I had six employers! I worked as a camp counselor, a kayak guide, and as a respite care worker for young adults with disabilities. I had regular shifts and was also on call 24/7. I said yes to every opportunity. By the end of the summer, I burned out. In hindsight, I realize now that this was adrenal fatigue. I didn't understand how badly I had damaged my body because it was my first experience with fatigue of this nature, and in my naivety, I brushed it off instead of listening to my body's needs.

FACE DOWN ON THE FLOOR

In my twenties, I continued to apply my love of hard work to every aspect of my life, especially school. I pulled countless all-nighters, polishing school assignments and studying. I was a perfectionist, and straight As were my goal.

It was during this time that I met my future husband. He was a bookstore manager and had a beautiful work-life balance that I could not yet understand. Shortly after we moved in together, he gave me one of the biggest lessons of my life.

It had been a long day at school. I was excited to return home to a warm embrace from my fiancé. However, when I walked in the door, he lay motionless, belly down on the living room carpet. I froze. Then my wilderness first aid training took over, and I sprang into action. I called out and was relieved to hear that he was able to speak. He was calm and assured me that nothing was wrong. This confused me. *Who in their right mind would purposely choose to just lie on the floor in this way?* If there was not anything physically wrong with him, then I decided that he must be deep in thought, working through something of concern. I pressed for answers. He continued to assure me that everything was okay and that he was just listening to music and relaxing. *Relaxing?* I could not comprehend. In my world, relaxing still involved doing something physical or mental; even meditating was an act of doing something. It would take over a decade before my understanding of relaxing would be forced to change.

After I finished school, we married, and three years later I gave birth to a beautiful baby girl. During the pregnancy, I was exceptionally nauseated and fatigued, and I struggled with insomnia. For the next two years, I experienced extreme fatigue but had many people tell me that it was normal to be tired as a parent. Consequently, I ignored how loudly my body was screaming at me to slow down. My fatigue worsened. I had struggled with fatigue since I was a teen and didn't understand that the intensity of the fatigue I was experiencing was not normal. One day, when my daughter was two, my fatigue became so bad that for eighteen hours, I drifted in and out of sleep. I was alone at home with my daughter. I could not keep my eyes open. I had experienced challenging days before but never one this bad. Recognizing that I would not make it through the day without accidentally dozing off, I made sure our home was safe, set my daughter up with TV shows to watch on an iPad, and made a bed for myself on the floor of her bedroom. Throughout the day, I drifted in and out of sleep. When I woke, I would check on my daughter to see if she needed anything. Multiple times I literally crawled to the kitchen to get snacks or food, then returned to her bedroom and drifted off to sleep again. Late that evening when my husband got home, I went back to bed. The next morning, I realized that something had to be seriously wrong with my health.

I went to the doctor and was diagnosed with adrenal fatigue and hormone imbalance. In learning more about adrenal fatigue and hormone imbalance, I realized I had multiple experiences of this in my past but had been unaware of it and fortunate in that my body was able to naturally heal itself. This time recovery was slow, exceptionally slow. At one appointment I asked my doctor why it was taking so long for me to recover. She told me I needed to slow down and if I didn't slow down fast, recovery would take a decade or more.

THE BRIDGE

During this time, we lived in North Vancouver in British Columbia, Canada. I worked part time as a yoga instructor and full time as a mom. My husband worked in the downtown core. Every day he would either run or take the bus to work. He worked long hours six days a week, and my daughter and I missed him. Sometimes we would drive downtown in rush-hour traffic to pick him up so we could spend extra time with him and then drive back in rush-hour traffic. The traffic on the bridge was horrendous at this time, and it would often take us an hour and a half to make the round trip. One day as we inched along in stop-and-go traffic, I thought about how silly it was that we lived in the city but were not able to enjoy the accessibility benefits of living in it. If we needed milk, I hopped in the car and drove to the store. We spent a lot of time in some form of transit. That day I decided enough was enough; if we were going to live in the city, then we needed to live close to my husband's work so we could spend more time together as a family.

I felt a constant tug at my heart to simplify our lives. After years of ignoring these whispers, I finally listened. The year before my daughter started school, we moved into downtown Vancouver. Our lives became richer with less time spent in transit and more time enjoying each other's company. We walked across the street and were immediately connected to the seawall to bike or skateboard to parks and an abundance of activities. If we needed groceries, we simply had to walk a couple blocks, and before we knew it, we would be home again. No more spending hours commuting. The first year of living in downtown Vancouver, our life slowed down to a more manageable, dare I say thriving, pace, and I saw a noticeable shift in my health. Living a slower life made an enormous difference. This was temporary. I had not yet learned the art of saying no to opportunities. At a steady pace, more and more was added to our lives.

INABILITY TO SLOW DOWN

For a while, life was simple again—we spent more time together as a family, we drove less frequently, and we embraced a life with less hustle. Slowly, our life picked up pace. The school my daughter was supposed to attend was at maximum capacity with long waitlists each year. A lottery system was used for student placement, and my daughter was sixty-fourth on a waitlist of sixty-eight children. The school she was placed in was a thirty-minute drive or bus ride away. Each day we commuted to her school in the mornings and then to extracurricular activities in the evenings and weekends. By the time my daughter was in second grade, she had made it into the school close by. However, every day of the week was filled with activity, and eating snacks, dinners, and lunches in the car had become our norm. There was rarely an evening without some form of extracurricular activity. She participated in gymnastics, Girl Guides, Chinese class, acting class, and she was a successful actress. Acting meant memorizing pages of sides for auditions and going to auditions all over Vancouver, and when she booked a role there were long, fun days spent on set. I wanted my daughter to have every opportunity possible, and she, too, wanted it all. My daughter worked and played hard, the same as I had always done. The cycle of doers continued. I had yet to understand that there was power in simply being.

By saying yes to every opportunity that came my way, my life was full, but it didn't feel whole or fulfilling. Every part of me craved simplicity and the ability to drop my shoulders and feel relaxed. The noise and chaos of doing it all and being it all blocked out my ability to enjoy it. Life outside our home was full, and when we came home, our house was so full of stuff that often we could not find what we needed at the moment. Something needed to change, and so began my long journey toward designing a happier life.

My health plateaued; there was no space to breathe and enjoy the little moments. Opportunities would come up, and I kept saying yes. It was my default response even when my whole body kept screaming a resounding no. My heart told me that I needed to slow down, but I did not know how to. I began reading books and listening to audiobooks about minimalism, simplicity, and creating a balanced life. I feasted on authors and people flooding the market with methods for creating a simple life.

I was determined to make the necessary changes to permanently bring back my health. I began researching and came across the three lifestyle concepts of minimalism, essentialism, and slow living. Each concept focused on consciously designing your life through the art of refinement. Living with fewer physical objects and activities gives space to live a life filled only with what makes you happy. The beauty of these lifestyles is that there is no right or wrong way of bringing them into your life.

> *Have nothing in your house that you do not know to be useful, or believe to be beautiful.*
> *—William Morris*

I dove into decluttering with great passion and excitement. It felt so great to be organized, but it only lasted a short while. While I was battling with clutter in my home, I was still battling with crippling fatigue and hormonal imbalances that often left me bedbound. On a day that I had energy, I would work tirelessly to clear the clutter from one area, only to become further fatigued and overwhelmed the next day. Then slowly, our home became filled again. This was a vicious cycle that repeated itself, but slowly over time, I was able to make permanent changes. In this journey of physical decluttering, I also learned how to say no to activities.

> *We can find our center of gravity within ourselves by simplifying and slowing down our lives.*
> *—Eknath Easwaran, Climbing the Blue Mountain*

My health once again began to improve, then the perfect storm hit. We became pregnant with our second child, nausea and fatigue once again ruled my world, and my parents sold my childhood home. I collected my childhood belongings and crammed a storage locker worth of items into our apartment. I was physically ill and beyond overwhelmed. My goal of bringing more into our lives through less now seemed like an impossible dream.

Determined to move past my feelings of overwhelm, I focused on my strong nesting urges and made a plan. I rented a storage locker, moved my childhood belongings into it, then focused on making a space for the little boy growing in my belly. I was motivated to continue refining our lives and was excited for the possibilities this would give our family.

2020

Then, at thirty-four weeks pregnant, my marriage unexpectedly ended. My world imploded. Seven weeks later, in mid-March, our son was born, and the world stopped. Everything came to a standstill—businesses, corporations, schools, the entire society and life as we knew it came to a screeching halt as the WHO declared COVID-19 a worldwide pandemic. There were pivots being made and everyone was doing their best to adapt and evolve, adapt and rise quickly. The new reality of what was happening in my personal life and simultaneously with the world was overwhelming.

> *Do not worry that your life is turning upside*
> *down. How do you know that the side you are*
> *used to is better than the one to come?*
> *—Rumi*

My life felt like a large purse whose bottom had just ripped open, strewing its contents on the floor. I was desperately trying to pick everything up but there was too much to carry and nowhere to put anything. I was forced to step back and assess the contents of my life and was given the opportunity to carefully choose what to keep and what to discard. Maybe if I gave myself enough space, I would have the capacity to add something new that I had always longed for.

With the ongoing lockdowns, I was given the opportunity to reassess my life. I enjoyed the moments that I had with my daughter and my second baby. We were not racing from one activity to the next. My son's first year was quite different from my daughter's. I watched him grow up from baby to toddler and was mesmerized at how present he was in each moment of his waking life. I decided to lean into my whispers that urged me to live more simply again. This meant being intentional and thoughtful of my choices—being discerning between what I said yes and no to—and helping my children to do the same.

What did I need more of in my life? What did I want to prioritize? I wanted time with my children that I could be present in. I wanted a home that was not noisy with things that needed to be taken care of. I wanted dinner time with my children where we could all sit down together and connect.

For most people, they choose to move to the country to quiet the busyness of life in the city. I am fortunate to live in a city where I can live in the downtown core and have access to everything. For me, living a simple life means saying yes to one or two activities and no to the rest. It is quieting the space that I live in with fewer physical objects and fewer things to do. Doing so helps me hear my inner dialogue and quiet the noise within too.

Feeling better than I had in years, I felt strong enough to start clearing out the excess baggage of my life that no longer served me: the emotional, psychological, and physical clutter. Saying no to the noise that limited me from living the powerful authentic life I wanted to lead with my kids was liberating. After a decade of having my life on pause, I was excited to begin living again and pursuing my dreams and goals. Most importantly, I was finally able to be the mom I always wanted to be: present, calm, and adventurous.

I decided it was time for a fresh start. Two weeks before my son's first birthday, I moved into a new apartment and began my new life with my two beautiful children. There was so much I wanted to do and so many paths to choose from. First, I needed to complete the huge task of decluttering our belongings in my home and storage locker. I wanted to pare down our belongings so that our home could be free from visual noise. I had a newfound motivation that I had never felt before but recognized that with a new baby, this would need to happen at a slower pace to prevent burnout. Second, I needed to rethink what I wanted my life to look like. It quickly became clear that I needed to change my career and go back to school. Third, I needed to give myself the time and space to process the many changes that had happened.

> *Desire creates more desire.*
> *The whole world goes on in this way.*
> *The silkworm makes a net to imprison itself.*
> *In the same way we make a net of attachments,*
> *desires, possessiveness around ourselves and we*
> *sit inside that net in pain and depression.*
> *As long as the net is intact the silkworm*
> *remains dormant, but as soon as it is broken the*
> *silkworm comes out in the form of a butterfly,*
> *which can fly and make everyone happy. In the*
> *same way, if we break our self-created net of*

*desires and attachments, we will become one
with our true nature.*
–Baba Hari Dass, *Silence Speaks: From the Chalkboard
of Baba Hari Dass*

Reflecting on these past two years, I can honestly say I have never been happier. I am more content, more focused, more determined. I find it easier to shut out the noise of the world so I can be more present in each moment. The calm that comes from living a life with less stuff, living slower, and focusing only on allowing what is truly essential in my life has brought happiness into my life in unexpected ways. I now have a calmer mind and the space to say yes to opportunities that I wouldn't have before, which allows me to be more present with my children and life.

That first year and a half after my marriage ended was the hardest I have ever faced, and I view it as the biggest yogic practice of my life. Thankfully, I had a strong support network and an even stronger faith. Whenever I felt lost, I refocused my energy back to my kids and repeated my mantra, "Everything happens for a reason." For the first time in a decade, I sat down and wrote out my life goals. Now that I was healthy, I was more determined than ever to chase my dreams and achieve them, but no longer at the cost of my mental, emotional, and physical health. And this time around, I'd allow my whispers to guide me. I'd listen to my body, I'd slow down when I needed to, and I'd speed up at a pace that honored me.

There will always be noise and distraction that will pull us away from living our purpose. But we hold the power. We get to decide exactly how our life story is written (to the best of our ability). Life can be as full or as simple as we choose. Like a buffet, we have a variety of incredible options at our fingertips, and it's easy to have the "shiny object" syndrome and choose too much and do too much. Living a simple life and listening to the whispers of our heart looks different for each of us. For me, this looks like living in a busy city with access to everything yet refining my ability to say yes to aligned opportunities that bring me peace and joy and saying no to anything and anyone else that doesn't feel aligned. It means taking time each week to do a life-happiness audit; this is my time to reflect and assess my path forward. It's my time to really tune in to the whispers of my heart so I can continue forging a life that is filled with joy for myself and my children. If you are ever doubting which way to go, what to do, and how you can infuse more of your desires into your life, start by subtracting the excess. Let go of what no longer serves you. Lean in, pay attention to your breath, your body, your heartbeat, and your energy—they will show you exactly what you need. Be discerning of what you say yes and no to. Make sure you aren't saying no to yourself and your overall health and well-being as a result. If you're waiting for permission to go live a life of abundance and happiness, let this be it.

Live simply.
Chase your dreams.
Say yes to what you love.
Say no to that which doesn't serve you.
Listen to the whispers of your heart.

Chapter 15

THE RISK TAKER

AMY MILNE

Being committed to your evolution requires being committed to your whisper.

@milneamyr

Amy Milne

Amy Milne is an award-winning event producer, marketing expert, entrepreneur, author, and speaker. Three years ago, she and her high school sweetheart of thirty years and firefighter husband, Eric, her two teen boys, Spencer and Jack, and Jake the killer cat, left the east end of Toronto for a new life in The Blue Mountains. Upon arriving at their new home, they adopted Bella, a rescue dog from northern Alberta, completing their family. With a home at the base of the ski hill and Amy's natural hosting tendencies, it was only fitting she open an Airbnb so she could share the beauty and fun of her new hometown with others. A born entrepreneur, Amy spends her days leading her teams at Beyond Inc. (an international marketing and event firm), Bea & Co. (a mobile trailer bar and staffing company), and The Pop-Up Event Company (a company she cofounded in 2020). The common thread here—all things events are her jam! Or cup of tea or a glass of wine . . . actually, all the things! When Amy is not producing life-changing, memory-making events or helping nonprofits raise more money by clarifying their message, you can find her SUPing on Georgian Bay, hiking up Blue Mountain (or skiing down it depending on the season), and, of course, indulging in Après with her friends and family.

IG: @MILNEAMYR

While I seek my own path, I am never alone on this journey. I have a fine collection of good humans I am beyond grateful for. Lucky for me, those who know me best know which parts of this chapter they share with me. Spencer and Jack, let my bold and brave decisions show you anything is possible and to always follow your intuition. Eric, thank you for walking with me. I love you.

Your story is what you have, what you will always have. It is something to own.
—Michelle Obama, *Becoming*

They say entrepreneurs are born, not made. I guess you could say this is true, for me at least. Without even realizing it or knowing it, at my core, I lived and breathed the traits of an entrepreneur. While not a risk seeker, I am a risk taker. And I am not afraid to stand up for what I believe in or do what most people wouldn't do. It never made sense to me when people often responded, "We can't" or "That's just the way it is . . . or it has always been done that way." I always wondered, *Why can't you do it your own way? Of course, you can. And if the path doesn't seem clear now, okay, you'll clear it, or it will unveil itself.* The unpopular vote, the off-beaten path, the avant-garde thinking has been one I have sought for myself for as far back as I can remember.

Whether it was on the playground or in the classroom, adults or kids, no one was free from my ideas on what was right, wrong, or possible. Looking back, I was always all about living for the possibilities, dreaming them up, and figuring out every next step as I went along. This was the piece that freaked people out the most, shook them up, made them think differently when they didn't want to—so when I was younger, I got shut down often. While for some, this would make them feel sad, defeated, like they should just give up, it did the opposite for me. In fact, it spurred me on. It ignited a fire within me that refused to be quelled. I wasn't afraid. And when I was afraid, I didn't let it stop me. Ever. I have lived my life *on purpose* and *with purpose* without regrets. Even after I have made a bad choice or unpopular decision, my reaction isn't regret, shame, or to shrink, it's to regroup, re-prioritize, learn, grow, and move on.

I grew up in the Beach, in the east end of Toronto, in a beautiful house on Brookside Drive. The street was lined with trees and filled with kids. We had a gate to Cassels Park direct from our backyard, so I spent all my summers ruining bathing suits by "swimming" around the cement wading pool and doing crafts with the park counselor at the hut. My parents worked hard; however, money wasn't enough. It was enough to ensure my sister and I had what we needed, but it didn't leave much for travel and vacations. One of the things I loved most about growing up in the Beach was knowing that every road south led to the lake. This was my version of a vacation, the place where I started dreaming and imagining how I would love to live.

Leaving my house every day for school, given we lived in the middle of a huge hill, meant I started the day gazing at the lake. There was something so calming and exciting about this at the same time. Looking out over the streets to the enormity of Lake Ontario meant infinite possibility to me. To me, it symbolized adventure and exploration. It meant leaving your comfort zone and believing in all the possibilities ahead of you. Just because you couldn't see the other side didn't mean something amazing wasn't there. It allowed me to start many of my days thinking about all the possible ways to get across it and where it might take me. Water has always played a part in my life. Like it is an actual friend or thing I need in my life. It brings me peace, joy, and a smile every time.

One of the coolest things about growing up where I did is that my Teta (Serbian for the mother's sister) lived right next door. She was a Canadian actress, singer, and a lady who did not live her life by popular vote. She was unpredictable, lived for adventure, and was quite progressive for her generation. She was incredible. She loved me and my sister so much. Everyone on the street thought she was so cool— they even called her Teta. Watching her live her life as she wanted was inspiring, and the best part was that she often included me. My sister and I didn't just get to go to the theater to see musicals and plays, we truly got to experience them—meet the cast and go backstage. It was the coolest thing ever!

In 1987, when I was thirteen, I got a taste for adventure firsthand. This would change the way I thought about where I would live for the rest of my life. While all my friends were getting jobs (or no jobs) in the city, I took a babysitting job working for two actors in the play my Teta was performing in in Muskoka for the summer. Not a friend or fellow teen in sight. Just me, and you know what? I loved it! In fact, I thrived! My friends didn't get it, and that was okay by me. I moved into her tiny cottage, away from my family and everything I knew. I would have my days to myself by the water, I'd babysit in the evening while everyone performed, and once Tovah was picked up at 11:00 p.m., I would hop on my bike over to the Gravenhurst Opera House and take on the role of pit boss for the post-show poker game until the wee hours of the morning. That summer was magical, and not what the typical thirteen-year-old would choose, at least not the ones I knew. Most teens wouldn't choose a location and an experience with a grown-up over a summer of relative freedom in the city with her friends and boyfriend.

I did. I chose to leave my friends and boyfriend behind. I experienced all the feels. It was a surreal feeling to teeter-totter between missing my family, my boyfriend, and my friends, while at the same time, not missing them as much. I missed their proximity. But being with my aunt in Muskoka, working and creating my own schedule, and being by the water exhilarated me! Besides, I knew that home was only a phone call and train ride away. I woke up every morning to a crispness in the air, a smell, a feeling, something I just didn't have at home. Something I loved and craved but couldn't put words to at the time. Here, I was surrounded by adventure every single day! It was simplistic, slow, but also powerful!

After that summer, I made it my mission to never have a summer in the city again if I could help it! I didn't know how it would happen, but I knew I would make it happen. Being away from everyone and everything I knew gave me a sense of independence I don't think I would have ever experienced if I hadn't started leaving home at such a young age. I liked being anonymous. At times, this made me feel incredibly lonely, and other times, it was calming, exciting, and refreshing. My instincts always told me that as long as I followed these pulls for adventure, these whispers to seek whatever my heart desired, I would always feel at home, at peace with myself.

Fast-forward, I did find my way back to Muskoka in high school, just as I promised myself. For the last two summers of high school, I worked as a housekeeper at the Muskoka Sands Hotel (now known as Taboo), cleaning rooms by day and partying by night! Summer of 1991 was a summer of big change for this seventeen-year-old. I broke up with my longtime boyfriend who, while a great guy, wasn't so great for me anymore. That summer, I lived my most carefree life. I experienced my first summer romance, I boated to work every day, met new friends, and took even more risks with myself than I ever had; I was away from the day-to-day struggles of living in a newly divorced family, and being in Muskoka (out of the city) on the water seemed to make life better, in every way. I was always able to see things so much clearer in the fresh cottage air. I felt more myself than I ever did. I could be who I was, unapologetically, in so many more ways than I could when I was in the city (or home). With this newfound clarity and confidence, I knew the next year would bring even more. And it did. In October 1991, I finally got Eric, the boy I had had a crush on forever, to notice me, and we started dating. If you ask anyone who knows us, they will tell you that Eric and I are high school sweethearts. But there is more to our story. It is true, we met when we were in high school. I had a crush on him before he even knew I existed. He was actually dating a friend of mine (gotta love high school), and I thought he was the most amazing guy. Lucky for me, my friend did not. And so, a note was passed, and the rest is history!

Upon Eric's graduation, he headed out east for the summer while I went back to my housekeeping job in Muskoka. We both had a passion for living elsewhere and away from home. Both sets of our parents divorced while we were in high school, so when we could leave, we did. Those years of change were hard ones. My summer was epic as it always was every time I was back in Muskoka. I lived in staff accommodation in Gravenhurst with a bunch of teens my age. Independence might as well have been my middle name—we fended for ourselves, which meant cooking, cleaning, getting ourselves to work each day, and learning to live as a team. It made me resilient, confident, and was character building. It served as the inspiration I needed for what I knew I was going to do next. My fire for adventure, possibilities, and living life unapologetically was roaring!

Upon my graduation, I decided I was moving to Banff. With or without a friend, boyfriend, family member, it didn't matter. I wanted to see the mountains, take a huge break from the life I knew, and just go. Despite our year apart (or fortunately for it), Eric and I were still together. He came back from his year of travel, so he, too, was ready for our first adventure together. I was the first to leave, so three days after I graduated, I arrived in Banff after a long and lonely journey. I followed the fiery whisper of my heart and left everyone and everything I knew and got on a plane to Alberta. I was promised an apartment full of roommates, and I was so ready for it, excited even! Well, that's not so much how it happened. I arrived at an empty apartment. I had one roommate who was never there—amazing and fun, right? Wrong! For this extrovert, this was my worst nightmare. Not to mention, when you arrive in Banff in June, it's still daylight until at least 11:00 p.m., and yes, the elk also hung out on my front lawn! I desired adventure, and this definitely was one! This was also one of the scariest, riskiest, "WTF did I do?" moments in my life thus far. I sat on the couch and cried. I had no one to talk to, the time change made it impossible for me to call home, and I was hungry and had no idea where the grocery store was or where anything in town was. I mean, I get it, I was new. Ten minutes later, my very hangry and growling stomach decided to show both of us who the boss was around here. And thank goodness! I wiped my tears, stopped the pity party briefly, mustered all my courage and bravery, and knocked on the door across the hall to ask for directions. Lucky for me, that room was filled with some of the greatest people I'd ever meet, and the rest was history. This seems to be a familiar theme in my life. Follow the whispers of adventure and desire with bravery, do the things most wouldn't dare do, and be rewarded in return for honoring myself and my intuition. For being the brave and daring one.

For marching to my own drumbeat.

Eric eventually joined me and we left Banff a year later, moved back to Ontario, got married, got the house and had the kids. We did the things that were expected of us—things that fall in line with the checkboxes you are supposed to check off as you grow older. Good job, check. Married to your love, check. Dream home, check. Kids, check. Eric and I experienced so much together from day one. We experienced our dreams, our milestones (as a couple and individuals), and, of course, all the bumps and edges that inevitably take place as part of our evolution individually and as a couple and family.

Fast-forward to five years ago—2016. Middle age is a real thing, people. And so is the midlife crisis. My husband and I emerged battered but not beaten from one of the toughest and most tumultuous times in our marriage. And when I say tough, I mean tough in all the ways that make you grow. Bigger. Better. Stronger.

We weren't headed into a new chapter, we were starting a whole new book. We were writing a whole new story. Starting fresh from page one. I did so much soul searching and growing during that time that it became very clear, very quickly, that what was next couldn't look anything like what it currently was. We lived on what we thought was the perfect street, in the perfect neighborhood with the perfect neighbors, and our friends and family were literally blocks away. Yes, we had built a life that I loved; however, it was time for something more. There was that whisper for adventure again. For possibilities, exploration, and a deeper, bolder desire to live the lives we really and truly wanted. And not just a bit more, a lot more. You could say that perhaps something was missing from our picturesque life in the city. But to me, there wasn't anything amiss. No, this was a calling, a calling for something that dreams are made of. A big, bold move. We emerged new people and what we currently had wasn't enough anymore. While it was amazing and filled us with joy, it was time for something bigger.

We often talked about what we'd do in retirement or once the kids had gone to university. We had just been through the most honest and life-changing moment in our relationship, and the world seemed to open to new possibilities. And so, we decided to take the conversation from what to do and when to what we could do now. I made the decision that we were not going to wait until retirement to live the life we wanted to live. We were going to carpe diem the heck out of this life and live the life we wanted to while we could. No one knows what the future holds—now is the only time we have.

Eric had a beautiful vision: We'd move to a specific street in The Blue Mountains, next to the resort and with an incredible view of the mountain. We'd be able to walk to the village and enjoy the peace and quiet when the tourist season was over. We'd have the village to ourselves along with the beauty of the mountains until it was time for everyone to return for the fun and adventure the area brought to many. I liked his vision; it sounded lovely. Amazing even. Except, I had zero, like no, connection to The Blue Mountains area. Still, the conversation kept coming up, and one beautiful evening in the hot tub over many glasses of wine, I turned to Eric and said, "Why not now? Why are we waiting?" Our eldest, Spencer, was graduating middle school in a year anyway, and my thought was: *We won't mess him up too much if we move when he is starting high school, right?* Our youngest, Jack, would be going into grade 5; it would be a great time for him *and* for us. We'd be living the life we were dreaming of now, not years from now. Like right now.

As you know by now, I am the risk taker. I make big, bold decisions in my business all the time, and in the past—my life. Given what we'd just grown through, it was crystal clear to me that the time was now. A few more glasses of wine and a couple more hot tub conversations later, we agreed. Let the house search begin! There is no harm in looking, right? Shortly after we made this decision, I spent a week in Mexico and, upon my return, drove straight from the airport to a cottage we had rented. A few days in, sitting lakeside, staring at the trees, taking in the fresh air, not having been in the city for a couple of weeks, my mind was 100 percent set—we were moving. There was no other option for me. It was time for more. Time to live a bigger life now. YES! We were going to do it. The only hitch was that Eric only wanted to live on one particular street. In other words, our entire move to The Blue Mountains hinged on finding a house on this one street (FYI, not one single house had been on the market in years on this street). As much as our mind was made up, and we were all set to move, this felt like a trick question or a pop quiz from the Universe.

Well, if you're someone, like me, who believes that the Universe always has your back, she had our back on this one. Within four months of making the decision to move, we were told about a house that was available on this exact street via a private sale! It was currently being run as a B&B, and the owner was motivated to sell to the right buyers. Of course, I decided *we* were the right buyers. Within moments of learning about this house, I managed to find their phone number, then called the owners. We had a lovely and meaningful conversation and made plans to come and see the home three days later. We came, we saw, we fell in love. Like madly in love with the perfectly decorated, 1980's chalet with carpeted bathrooms. We knew it was ours within mere moments of being in the house. By the time we left and were driving home, we decided it was time to call them and confirm we'd take it. Just like that, as we were turning left into Angus on our way back to Toronto, we made the decision to move to Blue!

At that moment, I was beyond excited. We knew we would be met with all sorts of thoughts and feelings about our decision given we knew most people never thought we'd do it, but we knew with our whole souls that this was the right thing to do for us and our boys. My first year there, I felt lost. Very much like how I felt when I first arrived in Banff all those years ago. I felt every emotion course through me. I lost myself. I felt like I'd given up so much of myself—my office, friends, business—to make this move. There was so much change, growth, doubt, and excitement. But eventually, we settled in and found our groove. We moved at a pace that exhilarated us and calmed us, a pace that finally made us feel alive—I'm talking full body alive—mind, body, and soul. No sooner did we start to find our groove than we were hit with another unpredictable moment, a moment that would require us to be so committed to our evolution, to our whispers, that any other alternative was no longer an option. The pandemic came in quickly, forever changing us for the better. Giving us the spaciousness, pause, and intentionality we needed to go within, to discover our joy and our adventure and start creating our own memories and writing our own stories anew in this beautiful place we now call home. Being committed to your evolution requires being committed to your whisper. And being committed to your whispers requires you to be radically courageous and to audaciously believe in the infinite possibilities your life has to offer you at every turn, every curve, and every moment in between. It requires you to be willing to break the ice, to do the hard things, to do what has never been done before so you can get to where you desire at a more aligned pace. The Universe is always whispering sweet dreams and desires to you; are you listening? She is always waiting for you to embrace your own rhythm and alignment and is forever conspiring in your favor. Are you willing to bet on yourself and your desires? Are you

willing to surrender to your fiery whispers and forge your own path?
No matter what?

Chapter 16

HOME

KIRSTI STUBBS

Look for the cosmic crumbs, listen to the whispers, love yourself enough to act on them, and allow yourself permission to live a life you love!

@kirstistubbs

Kirsti Stubbs

Kirsti Stubbs is an author, mental health advocate, personal brand coach, coffee connoisseur, intentional mama, and a woman on a mission. She is a corporate-ladder-climber-turned-entrepreneur who had that wake-the-fuck-up moment and never looked back! Through her writing and hosting the *Embrace Simplified Podcast*—with new episodes weekly—she guides other ambitious, badass women in becoming intentional in their wellness, relationships, business, life, and parenting. A bold storyteller, Kirsti openly shares the juggle of motherhood, experiencing burnout, and how prioritizing self-care allowed her to start playing bigger in her life. Join her on Instagram where she is slinging hope and authentic thoughts on life, loss, and learning to start over.

IG: @KIRSTISTUBBS

To my friends and family who have been there for me and my kids during all the change—your kindness means the world to me. Friendship isn't built in the big things—it's a million little things. It may seem small to ask me how I'm doing, to call on a Sunday morning, or to simply give me a hug, but when I was emotionally exhausted, your small thing kept me going. You are each a special part of my story, and I am forever grateful.

You are here to decide if your life, relationships
and world are true and beautiful enough for
you. And if they are not, you must decide if
you have the guts, the right—perhaps even the
duty—to burn to the ground that which is
not true and beautiful enough and get started
building what is.

–Glennon Doyle, *Untamed*

Nine years ago, I visited a little spot outside the city—in fact, the trip was a babymoon. That silly Instagram-named vacation you take before the baby arrives and you become parents. It was in an up-and-coming spot known for its food and wine scene. From the moment we exited the highway, I fell hard for the idyllic lakefront towns we drove through. It seemed like every other person we met had escaped the city and was embracing a simpler life. I looked at them in awe. We took cooking classes inside someone's home and learned to make sausages, and we sat around a big farmhouse table talking for what felt like hours about sourdough starters with the owners of the cooking school. The locals call this area the County, and although it rained all weekend long, I dragged my pregnant belly from restaurant to restaurant and enjoyed discovering and learning the area.

After that trip, I found reasons to visit the County a couple times a year because it always grounded me. One year I became extremely interested in following the County real estate market and campaigned hard for the purchase of an Airbnb property. The whispers were loud for me then, yet the external noise and chatter of others around me won out over my inner self, and sadly, we never purchased it. The cottage was listed at under $200k seven years ago, and at the time I am writing this chapter, it would be valued at well over $500k and has operated as a sold-out vacation rental for the entire time—plus, they haven't updated the building or changed a thing. *For the record, **that** would be one of those whispers with the neon lights that I failed to act on.* Let's just say it was love at first sight for me and the County—the lake, the wine, the shops, and the people all just felt like home to me. One trip away for a weekend turns out to be one of those cosmic crumbs of life.

Let's back up. In my twenties, I never consciously thought about checking off life's conventional success boxes. I merely went through the motions of doing all the things and being all the things to all people. Looking back, I can now see how, subconsciously, checking those boxes was a huge focus. I have never been afraid of doing things my own way but through standard conditioning, I had very outdated/traditional societal expectations for what we "should" do as we become an adult. By the time I turned thirty, I had most of those boxes checked off. However, they came with a lot of pressure, stress, and anxiety. It was like I finally managed to buy myself a really fancy, coveted pair of shoes that didn't fit right but I tried to push my feet in and grin and bear it because that was more socially acceptable than going barefoot. *Fashion over comfort, right? Who cares if you have to pretty much cut off all room to breathe in order to fit in. Who cares if you have to become an invisible shell of who you truly are, all to keep "them" happy.*

It turns out, I care. I turn forty this year and my life today looks quite different to what I had thought I was striving for in my twenties. One thing I will tell you, I did not see this coming. I didn't see myself as the woman who would ditch the fancy, coveted shoes to wander barefoot—carefree and boldly, courageously. Still, I wouldn't change any of it. Now, I love being barefoot, but I wouldn't have known that or discovered that had I not tried to fit into those fancy shoes.

I have known from a young age what it means to trust your intuition and that opportunities come your way for a reason. You need to lean in ("Grab them," as my dad would say), listen ("Block out what others think," as my mom would say), and have the courage to trust yourself and act (which I saw both my mom and dad do) because those nudges lead to extraordinary experiences and a life you love. My parents practiced what they preached. By simply watching them live their lives, I learned that variety in what you do is good, you can create a life that is different to others, and it is safe to change your mind. I took away that if it feels right, go for it. That inevitably, I hold the answers I need if I trust myself. If they wanted to try things, they did so without holding themselves back—open a business, change careers, move towns, save their money, spend their money, be generous to their community, start a new hobby, give their time to build something special . . . I can think of clear examples for each one, and many are in my most formative teenage years. My dad started a new career when I was young and that meant moving away from his extended family and moving us to a small island. My mom transitioned from full-time stay-at-home mom to student to hairdresser to entrepreneur when she turned forty. Even before I was born, she had a whole range of interesting jobs! They even took on building and operating a bed and breakfast long before Airbnb was a thing, which turned out to be the seeds of my entrepreneurial spirit. I now see that my self-trust in going for opportunities put in my path and deep knowing there is a bigger plan unfolding comes from my mom and dad. Now as a parent myself, I see what an amazing and precious gift they gave me—to believe in myself no matter what. I have seen how life circumstances and our own choices can lead us to self-betrayal or how life throws us unexpected things that test our self-trust. Through trusting their own intuitive nudges and living a life they loved, they also gave me permission to do the same.

I think we can all agree that it is hard to see the whispers and nudges for what they are IN the moment. It is a lot easier to look back at age twenty, thirty, or even now at forty and *really* pause and reflect and notice how the smaller moments have been connected and see the little cosmic crumbs the universe dropped in our path. They were the intuitive signs we needed to feel guided and nudged. And looking back to notice the moments we trusted ourselves gives us the confidence and reminder to trust where we are currently at is, in fact, where we are supposed to be. Something that should have felt scary felt settling and something that was filled with uncertainty somehow felt certain. That is our intuition with the volume up, even if no one around us understood it or it surprised us. I see now that sometimes it was a gut feeling, but it often seemed like blind faith, naïve hopes, or even romantic idealizations were in the driver's seat of the twists and turns in my life. Up until this point in my life, what I lacked in spirituality and surrender I made up for in hopes and dreams. And sometimes there were also not-so-quiet whispers (like sirens going off and neon lights blinking), and I still managed to miss them, ignore them, or just delay acting on them—I give myself compassion for those times too. I have earned each gray hair and wrinkle line. I am so proud of these markers, as they have given me the evidence I needed to trust that life unfolds in a way and pace it is meant to.

Remember how I said my life today is unrecognizable to my younger self? It goes both ways. I thought I knew myself then, but I was a reflection of everything and everyone else around me. I feel more ME now than I ever have—and my life now is something the twenty- and thirty-year-old version of me would not have ever dreamed. That is more than okay with me.

I have made bold changes in my life. When I meet people who hear my story, it's only when I see their reaction that I remember it's a big thing I have done. I forget that many still feel and allow the invisible shackles of the life they have built. A life they thought would fulfill them and the life they are afraid to leave now keeps them stuck in one place. I forget that I have always been someone who is not afraid to make changes, moves, or fresh starts.

At seventeen, I felt a loud YES to going on a student exchange that took me to Australia for a year. It gave me the gift of independence and confidence at a pivotal time in my young adult life.

At nineteen, I felt a loud YES to leave the island where I grew up and move into my first apartment with my best friend. It allowed me to discover the big city life I craved.

At twenty-one, I felt a loud YES to take the management position at the retailer where I had worked my way up. I started to take leadership seriously, and it forced me to take responsibility in new ways.

At twenty-three, when I felt a loud YES about moving to Vancouver and returning to school after four years working full time, I did just that. It gave me space to spread my wings and start fresh.

At twenty-six, when I felt a loud YES to moving across the country and starting a new life in Toronto, I leaped. That leap of faith led me to grow my career, meet amazing people, live in a diverse and exciting city, start a family, and eventually plant roots in a very special community.

I didn't know where any of these things would lead me when I jumped in, but they felt like the right next step. Some came with a lot of hesitation, others with a gut punch of a lesson, and some allowed me to meet the most amazing people, spark new passions, kick off my career, or discover how I could make an impact in the world.

It was in Vancouver, at age twenty-three, that I began lending my time to a nonprofit I was excited to work with. All those unpaid hours (and there were a LOT) gave me the feeling of purpose for the first time in my life, and I never questioned my time invested. It just felt right. Through that group I was introduced to many people who would play a critical role in how my life unfolded next: the person who hired me out of university, the mentor who would guide me to discover my biggest strength, the people who would teach me what friendship really looked like, and the man I would start a family with. It all seems divine now when I look back. . . .

Now, let me fast-forward and paint you a picture of my life at thirty. I had just bought my first home in one of the most expensive real estate cities in Canada. My spouse and I rode matching bicycles around our up-and-coming neighborhood when I wasn't working at my dream job in a large global Fortune500 corporation. I was recognized as a *Top 30 Under 30* in my industry, and I loved my job. I was also pregnant with our first child. And while my daughter grew inside me, we completed filming of an HGTV show where we renovated our basement with an income suite. I took beautiful vacations twice a year like clockwork, had a stunning wardrobe and shoe collection, and a large group of friends. I had it all, or so it seemed. I had been a "good" girl, and I went out and made the life that I thought I should make.

None of these things are bad unless they come at the cost of your mental health, emotional safety, and overall joy. I worked hard for the life I had built (and I also acknowledge that there was a shit ton of privilege that had a hand in there). I can look back now and be both extremely proud of what I accomplished and recognize that I was very unconsciously living my life. I was, without knowing it, checking off the boxes I thought I needed to check off in order to be seen as a "good, nice, successful" woman. In my first collaborative book, *Life, Love, Lemonade*, I describe a moment in my thirties as waking up and forgetting how badass I was. Once I remembered, everything changed.

Gradually, then suddenly, between ages thirty and thirty-eight, I completely lost my identity. I didn't see it coming. I spent far too long in survival mode and as an empath in a codependent relationship, that is a recipe for losing yourself. Through burnout and an unexpected caregiver role I took on, my sense of self got lost. I had stopped asking for what I needed, I let all personal and professional boundaries slip, and I fell into patterns of toxic femininity. Then, like a sour cherry on top, it all imploded with the kind of heartache and hurt that makes you distrust everyone, including yourself. Heartbroken, I was picking up the pieces of me and trying to put myself back together. Only this time, I didn't want to be put together the way I once was. This time, I was giving myself permission to ditch the checklist. Ditch the "I'm fine" and bounce back in ninety days, six months, or even a year. Did I "bounce back?" Yes, but in a way that felt true to me. I spent most of my thirty-eighth and thirty-ninth years giving myself the right to unplug, regroup, recover, and rediscover ME. And that permission I gave myself may be the single most important thing of my life. After years of being scared to even be seen for who I truly was, it would have been far easier/common for me to hide away in my pain. But I felt pulled to do something radical all over again, so despite my pain, I changed up our lives so that I could feel my best and leave the impact I wanted to make in the world. I left the community, friends, home, marriage, and work that I had carefully built around me and consciously put my life back together again in alignment with my self. This looked like evolving relationships by bringing back boundaries, nurturing myself with self-love, daring to dream, going to therapy, deepening friendships, and simplifying every single aspect of my life. Did I expect to lose so much in my journey to rediscovering myself and finding my own peace? Absolutely not. It was hard but worth it to give it all up to find myself again.

Now I am about to turn forty and I am back where the unraveling began. I live with my two amazing kids in one of those idyllic lakefront towns in the County that I fell in love with all those years ago. We moved here at the end of 2020, and I spent a year renovating the entire home and adjusting all of us to our new life. My marriage ended. I have been out of my corporate career for three years. The last two years of navigating the global pandemic and virtual school on and off have been interesting. Still, I feel more ME than I ever have. More certain, peaceful, and grounded than I ever did. I arrived in the County feeling shattered, and I got to "work" building a new normal for myself and my kids and doing all the unsexy work of learning to love and trust myself again. I have spent time intentionally creating a safe and loving home, listening and being the shoulder my kids could cry on, and reassuring them and teaching them to listen to their own whispers. We have all been through a lot of change at once, so right now everything else can wait. I put all my business dreams on hold to pour into myself and my kids (in that order), and I am starting to feel settled. I am proud of how I am building an unconventional life with a lot of intention. I shifted my focus to how I wanted to feel in my life and allowed those feelings to lead me. It wasn't an easy choice to make, but it was a rewarding one.

I will bet that if you sat down and made a list of all the times your soul has spoken to you and you've listened to its whispers, you will realize that it was all happening for you all along, even when the seasons of your life had storms, earthquakes, and massive upheavals. You will realize that you were being uprooted from everything you knew (and in some cases, initiating your uprooting) to bloom wherever you were destined to be planted and grow in an environment and direction true to you. When you listen to your intuition and make bold moves to change up your life, you will see how everything that led you up to that moment—all those cosmic crumbs—create these threads that are intricately woven together to help you discover the strength of who you are. And with it comes the certainty that life is unfolding (although often in the clumsiest way) just as it is supposed to.

If it doesn't feel right—that is your whisper.

If it feels very right—that is your whisper.

If it feels settling when it's scary—that is your whisper.

If it feels certain when it's an uncertain thing—that is your whisper.

Look for the cosmic crumbs, listen to the whispers, love yourself enough to act on them, and allow yourself permission to live a life you love!

Final Thoughts

Every minute of every day we are faced with decisions.

What to eat.

What to wear.

How to go ahead with a project.

Who to ask for help.

From the routine to the life changing, decisions are happening whether we are paying attention or not.

So, how do you arrive at your decision? How do you choose yourself and for yourself? In all the noise that surrounds us on a daily basis, how do you weed out what's important and what's just filler? Do you make lists? Weigh the pros and cons? Or do you listen to your gut?

Do you take that initial moment to pause and check in with yourself, your intuition, your gut instinct when you are faced with a decision and your gut gives you guidance? Do you follow that inner knowing? Can you even connect with what it feels like or have you moved past it so quickly that you don't even know when or if your body is speaking?

Sometimes ignoring those whispers creates bigger patterns that we only see when we take a moment to breathe. Our own inner guidance begins to give us more signs; for example, not wanting to do something or spend time with someone or saying yes to something that seems completely "out of character."

And yet that little inner guidance was there all along, tapping us on the shoulder, causing us to pause, guiding us to our true path.

Your intuition won't always roar; sometimes it's a soft sensation—goosebumps, chills, shivers. Other times it's the pounding in your head whenever you are around certain people, places, situations. Sometimes it's the pang of deep anguish in your heart. And other times it's that sinking feeling that you are steering away from your heart's compass, your inner knowing, and *whisper*.

Throughout this book, there have been themes of courage, boldness, softening and turning inward, and honoring the call for our inner adventure. Every story within this book shares profound and awe-inspiring moments when every woman honored her inner voice. Honoring your truth will require you to listen to the whisper of your heart. It will require you to be brave and stand for something instead of doing what is expected or what you think you should do. It will require you to drown out the chaotic and clamoring noises around you and to go within. Honoring your whisper is the most courageous thing you can ever do. Celebrate your moves, the challenges, the rise, the in-between, the unknown. Follow your desire, your fire. Ride the waves of your life. Take the path less ventured on; better yet, forge your own path. Be the lighthouse, the fortress, the sovereign stronghold who chooses herself over and over again. The woman who leads, loves, and lives in alignment with truth, her whisper, her intuition.

Make powerful waves, big, bold moves, and listen to the whispers of your wild soul.

Journal Activity

WHAT DOES YOUR INNER WHISPER TELL YOU? PAUSE, REFLECT, AND JOURNAL ON THE FOLLOWING QUESTIONS.

Complete these statements: I want… I need… I'm ready for… I let go of…

Connect back to a time when your whisper spoke to you. What did it feel like? Where did you feel it?

Connect back to a time when you followed your whisper. What was the outcome? How did it feel?

Connect back to a time when you didn't follow your whisper. What was the outcome? How did it feel? Did it shift anything for you?

Is there a common thread in how your whisper speaks to you? Is it your gut? Your heart? Your breathing? Something else?

Can you look back and see moments when you followed your whisper? What grew from that leap?

Do you want to try and tap into your whisper? Track the moments when your whisper is calling you, in the moment it's calling you.

Did you have a hunch or feeling about something and then it happened? What did it feel like in your body when it was a hunch? Did you follow it? Did you resist? What was the outcome? Have you experienced this hunch/feeling before?

Did you feel inspired to do something? An idea, creation, activity? Did you follow that inspiration and how did it feel? What was the outcome?

Did you experience any synchronicities or feelings of knowing? How did they appear? What were you thinking about at the time? Did they help with any decision or direction in something?

We often learn a lot from the things we didn't do. What is one big thing that you felt a whisper to do but didn't? What was the outcome? How did it feel in your body, mind, and heart? How did this situation affect other whispers that came after?

Do you feel different in your body when you follow your whisper and when you don't? Do you feel them in different places? Is the intensity or sensation the same or different?

Connecting to your intuition or whisper is a lifelong process that takes moments of pause and trust in yourself. These questions can be a starting point to help you tune into your inner knowing. Come back to these questions and revisit these stories anytime you need to tune into your inner compass and anchor deeply into self-trust. Trust the pull, the cosmic miracles, and the soft whispers of your soul's desire . . . welcome home, beautiful soul.

Works Cited

Chapter 3

The Seven Spiritual Laws of Success: A Practical Guide to the Fulfillment of Your Dreams by Deepak Chopra, 1994, Amber-Allen

Chapter 4

Animal Dreams by Barbara Kingsolver, 1990, HarperCollins

Chapter 6

Rising Strong: How the Ability to Reset Transforms the Way We Live, Love, Parent, and Lead by Brené Brown, 2015, Random House

Chapter 7

Year of Yes: How to Dance It Out, Stand In the Sun and Be Your Own Person by Shonda Rhimes, 2015, Simon & Schuster

Chapter 8

Lifetime Prevalence of Abortion and Risk Factors in Women: Evidence from a Cohort Study https://www.ncbi.nlm.nih.gov/pmc/articles/PMC7201453/, retrieved February 2, 2022

Chapter 9

Women Who Run With the Wolves by Clarissa Pinkola Estés, 2003, Ballantine

Chapter 11

Rising Strong: How the Ability to Reset Transforms the Way We Live, Love, Parent, and Lead by Brené Brown, 2015, Random House

Chapter 14

Climbing the Blue Mountain: Take the Next Step on Your Spiritual Journey by Eknath Easwaran, 3rd ed. 2022, Nilgiri Press

Silence Speaks: From the Chalkboard of Baba Hari Dass by Baba Hari Dass, 1977, Śrī Rāma Publishing

Chapter 15

Becoming by Michelle Obama, 2018, Penguin Random House

Chapter 16

Untamed by Glennon Doyle, 2020, The Dial Press

YGTMedia Co. is a blended boutique publishing house for mission-driven humans. We help seasoned and emerging authors "birth their brain babies" through a supportive and collaborative approach. Specializing in narrative nonfiction and adult and children's empowerment books, we believe that words can change the world, and we intend to do so one book at a time.

🌐 ygtmedia.co/publishing

📷 @ygtmedia.company

f @ygtmedia.co